a Nomad in Two Worlds

by
Ahmed Kemil
Mary Fallon
Doug Fallon
Cover illustrated by Dominique Q Gonzales
photographs courtesy Ahmed Kemil and Turmaline LLC

copyright © 2013 all rights reserved
ISBN 979-8-218-27906-6

Contents

Introduction

Mary and I first met Ahmed Kemil in 2009 when he enrolled in summer school at Brewster Academy in Wolfeboro, New Hampshire. The director of a non-governmental organization, *Rain for the Sahel and Sahara*, had approached us on behalf of a young man she was bringing to Boston for some medical services that were not availablein Niger. This organization partners with underserved rural and nomadic desert peoples of West Africa to help them realize their aspirations for education and durable livelihoods. Because the process was to take place over the course of a summer, she asked ifan arrangement could be made to provide him classes in English as a second language during his stay in the United States.

Ahmed is a Tuareg, one of the nomadic people of the Sahara in Niger, Africa. His story was compelling for many reasons and we felt the American and international students in our program might benefit from learning about his nomadic Muslim background. Perhaps Ahmed could be an ambassador of good will and give the otherstudents another perspective.

He did, indeed, prove to be an excellent "ambassador." Ahmed was universally loved and embraced by everyone at the school: students,staff and faculty alike. At the end of the program he received the Faculty award for the best all-around student. It was the first time thefaculty vote had been unanimous. No other student was even nominated that year.

As part of the program, each student at the Academy was provided aloaner laptop with Internet access. Ahmed, who hadn't even used electricity in the Sahara, was able to quickly blossom into a savvy IT consumer. Consequently, we were able to easily stay in touch with him after he returned to Niger. We followed his progress as he left his mother and siblings and lived in the capitol city, Niamey, to attendand eventually graduate from high school. There, he was able to use internet cafes to stay connected and hone his computer skills. At thetime, we considered this a convenience that was allowing communication that, otherwise, would have been difficult at best. ButAhmed was beginning to move inexorably into the second of two worlds.

Very few Tuaregs get a formal education. They are hard-working people, but most of the time they opt to stay in the desert, living as pastoralists, attending to their animals and moving frequently to findwater and pastureland. Ahmed was different. He saw that uranium mining, modern development and the southward advance of the Sahara (several miles per year on average) had an effect on the water supply and pastureland that increasingly threatened the Tuaregs' nomadic life. Their traditional territory was being squeezedon several fronts. Without water and pasture for themselves and their animals, his people either would not survive or would be forcedinto the cities of the second poorest country in the world. Ahmed thought that an education might allow him to help his people to be able to maintain their livelihoods and ancient lifestyle.

How could a nomad with no money, from a country that is so poor that 60% of its money comes from foreign aid, hope to advance his education and achieve a position of sufficient influence to be able to help his people? Mary and I, wanting to help in a worthy cause, agreed to host him for a year on a travel visa. During his first year in the United States, we felt that we could provide him with competencyin reading, writing and fluency in listening and speaking English. As retired educators, we had the necessary skills, along with a rare opportunity to be able to work with him one-on-one. We hoped that his developing a proficiency in English might aid him in somehow realizing his goal of getting a university education in order to return to Niger and be able help his people with water and other projects.

As part of his English instruction Ahmed wrote this book. While this may seem like a lofty goal for an ESL student who had only been in the United States for six months, he has worked hard to accomplish it. He wrote and re-wrote every day. Aided by his natural ability for languages (he speaks five), he has produced what you are about to read.

We didn't begin this process with the idea of actually publishing a book. The plan was to corroborate in a two-step process. First, I would work with Ahmed on grammar, syntax, usage, vocabulary building and colloquialisms. This resulted in many revisions. Afterward, Mary worked with Ahmed on re-writing everything in order to teach him to write with greater clarity. Mary helped Ahmed to describe the details. The prompt we used was simply to ask Ahmed to describe the most surprising differences he was seeing in comparing his experiences in the United States with those in Niger and to illustrate those differences with stories that would personalize those experiences. Because we spend winters in Scottsdale, Arizona, Ahmed was able to experience both the Northeast coast and the Southwest of the United States.

The idea to publish this book came a couple of months into the process. Mary and I began to notice that we were being drawn in more and more to the stories that Ahmed was writing as we learned about life and survival in the Sahara. We had friends and neighbors over to meet Ahmed, view his pictures from home and hear about his stories. It was after one of these gatherings the idea of the book began to evolve. At first, it seemed a far-fetched idea: an ESL student, with limited language experience, publishing a book in English. As we continued to work with Ahmed, however, we realized the piece had passed some basic criteria for a good book: it was interesting, compelling and we were learning from it.

Such an endeavor necessarily required collaboration, but Mary and I attempted to ensure Ahmed's book is a genuine and faithful accounting of his story. It is a story of his memories as a Tuareg youth and of his recent experiences traveling and living in the United States. His observations and insights while here in the United Statesallowed him to draw comparisons and conclusions from both. Our role was to help in that process by arming him with the tools of English so that he could record his stories and observations. Although Mary helped to frame some of the expressions; the experiences, observations and opinions in the following chapters are Ahmed's.

Doug Fallon

Mary Fallon

PART 1.
a Nomad in Niger

Losing an Eye

It was during the afternoon. My cousins and I, stood in a dusty stretch of ground in front of the small camels. The valley in which wewere herding the camels was a nice area with much grass and a fewacacia trees. I was 7 years old and our responsibility in the division of labor within the community was caring for the young camels. We had to keep them separate from their mothers because they would seek out the mothers' milk. In order to get milk for our families we had to separate them for the whole day, or we might starve.

The small camels were calmly feeding on the grass, yet seeking theopportunity to escape from us. We were playing in the dirt, our faces covered with dust, and none of us had shoes. One of my cousins was half naked in his blue pants that were torn apart. The atmosphere was hazy due to the sand kicked up by the goats andewes that were coming in from the pastureland to go to the tents. From time to time, we had to shoo the small camels back with ourchants "hyrric."

When we had first set up our camp, the young boys dug small holesas deep as a cubit and attached a stone or a piece of wood to secure ropes in the sand. When it was time to secure the small camels for the day, we used these ropes. Once the small camels were tightened in their ropes, we were finally free, finally free to playour games.

There were six tents in our camp, each one 500 yards from the other. The game that we were playing is called "balouss." It consists of tagging a person and running away quickly so he has to chase you down to tag you in return. We say if you are not able to touch theperson in return, his touch will infect you and you will sustain an "abous" or injury.

As we chased one another, my grandfather stood in front of his tent,wearing a long, black tunic. It was just before sunset, after prayers, and it was his meditation time. He walked up to us and called out "bararan-bararan." Immediately, we ran toward him and held out ourhands. He dipped his fingers into his palm and moving from one of us to the other filled our extended hands with sugar. I looked at my grandfather. He had wrinkled cheeks. His left eye was slightly closedand he had a white beard and white eyebrows. He always wore black, a black turban, a black tunic and traditional black pants. Despite the harshness and the burning of the sun, he maintained apale and delicate complexion. It gave a special "poetry" to his person.

Whenever he dealt with us children, he always had a gentle smile. On this day, his mouth and his smile were uncovered which was unusual. As a Tuareg male, he usually covered his face. That was our tradition. But here, among us, at this restful time of day, he was able to show that caring and gentle visage encouraging us to respect the quiet and tranquility of this time of day.

My people have always offered sugar as charity as is recommendedin Islam. Sugar was precious to us at that time, because we made candy out of it. We knew a little bit about commercial candy. Whenever someone in the neighborhood or in the family went to town, he would bring back some dates or some manufactured candyfolded in paper. That was how we got the idea to make candy out of sugar.

We used two different techniques to make our own version of candy.According to one version, we used a piece of paper which we rolled into a funnel shape. Then we cooked the sugar in a large spoon on the coals and poured it into our paper funnel. After allowing it to dry for a moment, we would tear the paper away and enjoy the sweetness of our "candy." Using the other method, we would first cook the sugar on the spoon as before and then pour it onto a stick which was resting on the surface of a plate so that the melted sugar would form a circle, our version of a lollipop, which we could suck onwith delight. To us, our desert candy and the candy from town tastedthe same.

That day, as we were finishing making our candy, we heard a low rumble moving toward us. We looked up and saw a white car trailinga cloud of sand behind it. We all stared at it in fear. We were not familiar with cars and to us it looked like a mechanical monster moving through the desert. The car stopped to the west side of our encampment.

As we huddled around the wood fire, my uncle who had been standing before his tent waiting to milk the returning camels, walked slowly and purposefully to the car. When he reached the vehicle, he extended his hand toward the open window and shook hands with the occupants. He then turned back to his tent, to a goatskin suspended on a pole in which he kept his supply of water. He filled abowl and carried it carefully back to the car. He handed it to the driver through the window as other occupants of the car began to climb out and step onto the sandy surface.

We kept staring at this scene, wondering what was happening. Thenwe watched our uncle turn from the car and walk toward us. As he neared, he began to explain to us what was happening. He told us that the visitors were here to give us drops to help us resist a seriousdisease, polio, which was present in Niger. "Don't worry," he reassured us. "All it is is a drop on the tongue." But some of us were immediately wary and three of us turned to run and hide behind the dunes.

The four of us who remained looked back at the car and the professional looking people who were standing around it. We recognized there were three nurses with the driver. "Follow me," ouruncle said and gestured to us to follow him to the car. We were frightened. We trusted our uncle, but we really didn't know what to expect from these people.

By the time we arrived at the car, our worst fears became a reality. We saw one of the nurses pull a box from the car and open it. Then he drew from it a hypodermic needle which he raised up into the air. When we saw the needle, we tensed and made ready to run away, but the other two nurses and the driver had blocked our passage andgrabbed us by the arms. We were all crying and calling out for help, but no one came to our aid.

One of the nurses held my arm securely and another slid the needle into my forearm. I felt the sting and prick of the vaccine as the nurseshot it into me. I began screaming in fear more than in pain. He thenn slid the needle out and swabbed my arm with antiseptic. What was happening to me was also happening to my friends. Finally, they released us and we stood in shock as the nurses climbed back into the car to rush on to the next camp.

It was getting dark and they were in a hurry to arrive at their next location before blackness descended. In their haste,

they left the boxof used needles under a tree, neglecting to
burn it. My uncle, who had been waiting to milk his camels,
had already hurried away fromus, and we were left there
looking at that curious box.

One of my cousins picked the box up from under the tree
and brought it to us. We opened it and peered inside. As we
examined the contents, the three friends who had
"escaped" the inoculation returned, wanting to share what
we had discovered. However, one ofmy cousins objected.
He pronounced that only those who had been injected
could claim and play with one of the needles.

I picked up one of the needles and looked at it. I saw the
measurement marks on the rubber syringe. They looked
beautiful tome. I had no idea what they meant. Now, it was
time to play. There,next to the box, was the bowl of water
my uncle had carried to the car. We knew what we wanted
to do.

Each one of us stuck our needle into the water and filled
it by drawing on the syringe. One of my cousins was
trying to shoot thewater out of the needle and was
having difficulty because air was blocking the stream.
We all gathered around him trying to make suggestions
until finally he shot both the water stream and needle
upinto the night sky. It was like a missile shot. The
ejected stream and needle made a popping sound.
Then we all looked up into that night sky which was
almost black and searched for the projectiles.

A few seconds later, I felt a stab in my left eyelid, a sting, a
prick andthen a drag which stretched the lid and penetrated
my eyeball. I screamed out in pain and fear and turned to
run to my mother's tent.My friends all ran after me as we
ran to the entrance. When I passedthrough the fan of reeds
that were woven together to keep the goats from entering,
my mother emerged asking what had happened. "Take it
out. Take it out," I called to her pointing to my eye. "What is
it? What thing?" she shouted fearfully cupping my chin in
her hand. She had carried a flashlight with her and now

used it to light my face.Seeing the needle, she yanked it out with her fingers. I felt the release of pressure and the relief of pain. I thought I would now be alright.

That night I lay on my mother's bed in the darkness. I was feeling a slight vibration in my eye. It was uncomfortable, but I didn't feel that itwas serious. As I lay there, I heard the voice of my grandmother approaching the tent. When she stepped closer, I could smell the scent of leaves and roots, the herbal remedies that she used in her role as a healer. She called my name and stepped close to the bed picking up the flashlight my mother had used. She sat next to the bed and examined my eye with the light. "You must come with me now to my tent. We must try to heal this wound… now." I climbed outof the bed and followed her to her tent.

I sat on her bed which was outside her tent as she went inside to collect her healing remedies. When she got back, she put the bag onthe other side of the bed, and then before she used the medicine, she leaned over me and licked the wound inside my eye to get rid of the poison. After that, she picked up a small quantity of pounded herbs in her fingers and mixed them with water. When the mixture was ready, she applied it delicately to my eye.

I felt a coolness. "Keep your eye closed now," she suggested, "and don't squeeze it." Then she gave me a mixture of herbs and medicines she had retrieved from a cloth and mixed with water. I took this by mouth. It was bitter. She told me to stay on her bed lyingon my back. After that, my neighbors came by to check on me and ask how I was. Now I was feeling fine. I thought everything would turn out well. However, the next morning when I woke up, I started seeing a black spot whenever I blinked my eyes. My left eye started itching very badly. When this happened, my grandmother would lick my eye with her tongue, and I felt some relief. Unfortunately, in reality, my eye was getting worse and worse as the poison was melting into it. The pain, the irritation, and the blackness were all increasing.

During the second day, my mother decided that we had to seek medical help. In order to seek that help, we had to travel to the nearest town which was forty-three kilometers from our camp. Therewas only one vehicle that traveled to this town. In order to meet up with this vehicle, we had to intercept it in its path in the desert whichwas nearly ten kilometers from our camp.

We set out in the morning for the site and waited through the first day, but the vehicle didn't arrive. At night we returned to our camp and then repeated this process for the next six days. On the seventhday, mother decided we had to find an alternative way to travel to town. She packed some food and water and we climbed on our donkeys. Since my mother was afraid and worried about the nights we would have to spend on our journey in the desert, she asked hercousin to accompany us on his camel.

In the meantime, my eye became more and more painful and I feared it would fall out. It was hurting so much, I could not sleep through the night. We left early in the morning of the seventh day. We had to spend the hot hours of the day under a tree and travel in the mornings and late afternoons on our animals which carried waterand food. It took a day and a half to reach the town.

As we rode into the town of Arlit, my eye was so irritated and painful I could only feel, not actually see, the activity of people around me. Itwas the first time I had been in a city. We first traveled to an animal market where we could leave our camel and donkeys and then we
walked to the hospital. I had never been in such a place. There wereno tents, only houses. Many electric lights illuminated the area around the hospital where the French employees of the huge company, Areva, lived. Everyone was speaking French, which my uncle and mother could not understand. Fortunately, my mother did speak Hausa which is understood anywhere in Niger. Therefore, when we reached the hospital, she was able to ask for help and explain to the doctor what had happened.

At the entrance of the hospital, the guards told my mother's cousin that he could not enter with us, but had to wait outside. Primarily, thishospital served the needs of the French occupants of the area who had been extracting uranium from the native resources for nearly forty years. Only occasionally, depending on the advice of individual doctors, did they serve the native peoples. As we entered the single-story building, I was overwhelmed by the smell of disinfectant. However, my primary concern was the intense pain in my left eye. I held a piece of cloth my mother's cousin had torn from his turban to my eye socket. I could barely see now with only my right eye functioning. A doctor in the reception room directedus to his office door and told us to wait for him. We passed into his office and we sat down in a line of chairs that occupied one wall. Thedoctor's equipment was located on the opposite wall, and we waited for his entry.

A few moments later, he entered from another door and asked my mother to explain my condition. She started explaining in Hausa as he stared at her. When she finished, he guided me to an automatedchair. I sat in it stiffly, my head up and my body rigid. He raised the chair I was sitting on and moved an optic machine close to my face.He examined my eye through one of the lenses, and then he removed the machine and looked directly into my eye with something like a flashlight. I stared straight ahead, still feeling the pain in my eye. As he folded his light, he leaned back from me and made the pronouncement to my mother. "You've come too late. His eye is already completely destroyed."

My mother, in shock and grief, explained to him why it had taken us so long to reach the hospital. The doctor reacted with compassion, shaking his head and looking down at the floor. He seemed to really care about us. He told us we should stay in the hospital in a room hewould assign and every day he would come to check my eye again. We stayed for many days, and he came every day to check on me.

However, the eye was already lost. We knew this because the irishad liquefied and was now seeping from my eyeball every day. It seemed to be melting. My left eye was lost.

While we stayed in the hospital, my mother's cousin would return tothe animal market, where his friend was a trader, to cook our meals.He would then carry the food back to us every day. His friend lived there in the market in a straw hut. He was a Tuareg who had movedto the city after a drought had killed all of his animals. The two men had retained their friendship from the desert, and this relationshiphelped us survive the hospital stay.

At the end of my stay, the doctor gave us some drops and some medication. My mother, her cousin and I returned by donkey and camel to our camp. And I continued my life with only one eye.

Sand Storm

My people, the Tuaregs of the Sahara, are pastoralists.
We breed camels, goats and ewes. In the desert, from
the oldest to the youngest, all members of the family are
assigned responsibilities toassure our survival. Usually,
young boys take care of camels and young girls take care
of goats and ewes. I was just 10 years old when the
desert taught me what it means to "take care of..." It was
one of the most important lessons of my life.

My three cousins and I had just taken over the larger
camels as wehad previously taken care of the smaller
camels when we were seven. This was an important
transition, and we were dedicated to fulfilling our
responsibility. On that day, it was my turn to lead the
camels to the well where members of the family were
filling their goatskins full of water to carry back to camp.
The well lay at a distance of about 20 kilometers in the
desert. I was leading the camels alone. I rode my camel

behind the herded camels. I wastaking care of them. It was between the dry and rainy seasons in the desert, and there was a slight sprinkle falling on us. During this season, the desert is unstable. According to my grandfather, this instability and the subsequent whirlwinds that spun over the sand were caused by a struggle between the two forces which the French call "l'armentant"and "la mousson." When I attended the French school, I learned to associate these two terms with the opposing forces already identifiedby my grandfather.

As I was riding alone herding the camels before me, I noticed that the weather had indeed become highly unstable. It was a very windyday, and from my experience, I knew that these winds could blow upterrifying storms that looked and felt like the end of the world. A few kilometers away from home, I saw that a huge, red storm cloud in the east was building. I could hear the low rumble of thunder in the distance. But I observed that my entire herd was chewing calmly on the grasses to swallow and regurgitate them, so I didn't really worry as camels have instincts about the forces in nature. Besides we have a tradition in our culture that tells us that often the red sandstorms, although they look frightening, mostly end up as what we described as the "sagging fat of an old hag, harmless and powerless."

Therefore, on that day, I thought the gathering storm was not going to blow strongly or become dangerous. I kept pressing ahead in spiteof the first gust of wind, but I put my turban on just in case. Almost everyone wears a turban in the desert, in order to protect their headsagainst the wind and the sun. As I was swinging around to check theweather front to my east, the storm started blowing. I could see that the huge red cloud had settled over the mountain and had now obscured it from my view. All that was visible was a huge bank of dust that had risen up to my right side as we traveled south. Would this be only a passing swirl or could it become something much much more threatening?

I could feel the fear rising through my body. My hands were shaking and I had to struggle to keep hold of the ropes I was using to guide the animals forward from my own camel. I started singing in order to escape from my fear, but at the same time I knew that sometimes if the wind starts blowing in the desert, it won't stop for two or three days. I also realized that here I was, out with the camels in my charge, and I had not prepared myself for a possible emergency. I had planned to obtain water at the well we were traveling to and had not provided for an emergency by carrying water with us from our camp, a terrible mistake in this desert climate. As we moved forward,the storm grew in intensity and began to engulf me. Now, when I held my hand up before my eye, I could not even see between my fingers. The air had become a red color and the wind was growing stronger and more fierce. How could I protect my flock? How could I protect myself? I knew I had to act. I had to find a way to survive.

I jumped down from my camel without waiting for him to crouch. After I had slid down his haunches, I tried to take control of the othercamels. But they kept moving ahead slowly while I struggled to stop them. I had made a plan that I hoped might save us. I needed to gather the flock around me and to place myself in the middle of the flock to take cover from the heavy and painful sand and the intense,drying wind. I knew the herd could offer me some protection and, in turn, I would be there to guide them.

I finally was able to stop the flock by heading them off with a raised stick. They instinctively turned west away from the force of the wind,and I was able to sneak in between them so that they actually formed a protective circle around me and my camel, Kaoda. As I leaned in against Kaoda's chest, even within the circle of camels, I felt the fierce pricking of the sand against my exposed skin and pulled my turban over the eyesocket of the eye I had already lost. I buried my face against Kodak's rough hide and hoped that somehowwe could survive this terrifying and powerful act of nature. I knew others had perished in the desert in storms like this one, and I wasalmost breathless with terror before the surge of wind and sand I was now experiencing.

It seemed as if hours had passed as I huddled there pasted against Kaoda, seeing nothing but a screen of deep red and black, hearing only the roaring wind that filled my ears, and feeling the force of pelting sand whipping against me. I felt my lips cracking in the dryness. My throat seemed to grow tight, and my head felt light and unstable. I was growing dizzy and disoriented. Trying to pull inside myself, I kept reciting a few paragraphs of the Koran which containsprayers to recite when in difficulty. There was little else I could do, but wait out the terrifying situation.

Then, after what seemed like hours in the torrent, little by little, I began to sense a change in the wind, a diminishing power in the surge that was blowing against us. In effect, the storm was beginningto move away from us. I raised my head and now could see some forms through the sandy air. As the wind began to moderate, I decided to lead my animals again. Unfortunately, I had lost my senseof direction and then, suddenly, the storm once again began to increase in intensity. I felt the wind once again whipping against me and said to myself, "Now I have to be careful not to be scared."

My biggest problem was that I wasn't carrying any water with me andthat kind of wind kills people all the time by dehydrating them. I was gripped with fear and was losing hope that I would survive. I was angry at myself for making such a critical mistake. I had told myself that I would get water at the well and had failed to carry any with me.Here I was without water and without hope. Now, I made a critical decision. I left the camels because I knew they would find the well bythemselves. I decided I would try to reach home on my camel. I turned Kaoda back north, and we began to trudge through the desert. Then I saw an astounding sight. I couldn't believe my eyes. There before me I saw my uncle in the red swirl of wind and sandwaving from his lovely white camel, "Edagnass." He had seen the gathering storm and had decided to come looking for me, carrying water with him. As our camels neared one another, Ibreathed very loudly and greeted him with joy. I grabbed the cup he was extending to me and leaned over to the side of his camel to spillwater into it from his goatskin's bag which was slung across Edargnass' back. I raised the cup to my lips and let the water slidedown my dry throat. I could feel the coolness and the relief immediately.

My uncle told me to go back home and promised me he would lead the other camels back to our camp. I knew I could trust him becausehe was a great guide in the desert. He used to lead a caravan from Niger to Algeria to sell camels and to buy food. I was greatly relievedas I left him and headed back home.

Soon I felt the wind easing, and I knew I would be safe from thestorm. On that day, I realized how dangerous nature could be despite how much you may love it. I had set out into the desert without carrying water with me. Because of my mistake and my failure to obey the rules of nature, I might have died. Even now if Ithink about that day, my heart beats more strongly. However, I appreciate every terrifying minute of that experience as I learned how to be more responsible and how to truly "take care of my responsibilities." That desert storm taught me well.

School in the Desert

Most of our classrooms in Niger are made out of straw.
However, wedo have a few classrooms built by foreign
NGOs. Those classrooms are made out of mud, and they
mean a lot to students because they last for a long time.
Many times, straw classrooms burn up or get destroyed by
sand storms. Sometimes we build another classroom ifwe
get enough straw together in a new area. To teach in the
desert is a challenge for teachers. Because we are nomads
constantly moving to seek water and good pasture,
teachershave to follow us to keep up with their students.
Whenever we start moving, there is one camel available for
the teacher on which to load his luggage and the

blackboard as well. Teachers often feel very isolated from the modern world and from their friends. Also, most ofthe teachers come from the south of Niger where water is available.Then there is the language. Many do not speak Tuareg. That's why some teachers don't want to go out of cities and teach in the desert.

I still carry in my memory the first time my mother took me to school.It was a distance of nine kilometers from where we lived. All my cousins with whom I went to school were excited to go except me.They were eager to learn new things and to learn how to read.However, I was nervous and afraid of being away from home.

On the first day, my aunt and my mother took me on a donkey's back. I was crying and jumping off the donkey whenever I could to escape from them, but they were able to drop me off into the hands of the teacher. I remember, as we approached the school, my motherand aunt tied the donkey to a tree. They also threatened me. "If you don't shut up and behave properly, we will tell the teacher to beat you with his whip." I was terrified.

As we walked up to the one-room stucco building, I saw that some students were returning from the well where they had gone to wash.We asked them where the teacher was, and they directed us inside.
The teacher, wearing a white turban, was sitting at a small table writing on paper. My mother and aunt greeted him and they all shookhands. Because there was only one chair in his "office," he suggested they drag one of the student chairs up to his. I looked at him in fear. I was terrified of being beaten with that "whip."

When we were seated, the teacher asked my mother and aunt why they had to bring me to the school rather than sending me there withthe other students. They explained to him that I had resisted, so theyhad to accompany me.

Then the teacher turned to me. Fortunately, he was a
Tuareg. Wewere able to understand each other easily.
In some schools in thedesert, teachers are from other
regions, so they don't speak Tamasheq, and this makes
it very hard for students to understand what they say.
The teacher tried to calm me down by advising me
about the importance of education. He said to me, "The
school will benefit you before anything else. Without
education, you won't be able to do anything in the
future." I didn't really listen to him, as I wasthinking
about escaping from school to go back home.

In the afternoon, my aunt and mother left school to go back
home. I was left there to adapt to and accept my new
situation. It was a big tragedy for me to leave home for the
first time. I spent the whole daycrying and figuring out how
to flee without being seen by the teacher.

We spent two weeks at the school without going home. At
first, I hated being there. By the fifth day, the teacher tied
my ankle to another student who did not like being there
either to keep us from escaping. We were separated from
other students, and the teacher placed a mat close to his
own straw hut for us to sleep on while we remained tied
together. He asked the cook to watch us through the night.
The cook would check us every hour with his flashlight. We
felttrapped, but we were determined to escape. Later that
night, because our hands were free we were able to loosen
the rope and escape.

We walked cautiously away from the teacher's hut toward
the desert,but the white shirt of my companion glistened in
the moonlight, and our footsteps made little padding sounds
in the sand. The cook eventually caught up with us with his
flashlight. He waved the flashlight on our legs as we ran and
the fluctuating light caused us tolose our balance. We fell
several times, but got up to run again and managed to
travel nine kilometers to the home of my partner. Soon word
of my escape reached my mother, and she traveled again to
find me and take me back to the stucco school. She warned

me thenthat if I tried to escape again, she would have the teacher lock me up.

After that experience, I did not try to leave again and little by little, I began to grow used to life away from home. We slept each night in astraw hut. The only meal we ate was millet, which we ate in the evening. Often there was nothing to eat at lunchtime. Almost all ourfood was given to us by the USAID through the government.

One weekend the teacher told us that we could go home if we promised we would come back to school. It was a very welcome dayfor all of us. I was excited about returning to our camp. We went to the well to grab some donkeys and planned to race them toward home. It was a Friday afternoon in December. There were only four thirsty donkeys standing around the well while there were six of us. We gave the donkey's some water and rode two donkeys with two people on each one. We left school before the sunset and got homejust as it was getting dark. We were like heroes. Everybody in the neighborhood came to see us. They asked questions about what wehad learned from school during the first two weeks. Fortunately, we knew how to count from zero to twenty. It was a very exciting weekend for us.

Early Monday morning, we were told that we could ride our camels back to school in order to be able to return each day after classes. Since it was still December, it was very cold when we left home! Wewere freezing on our camels, but fortunately we had our turbans on to hold the heat. On the other hand, the camels didn't feel the cold. They were just walking along slowly until we decided to race them ina flat area. We were having fun. As usual, we enjoyed being together. Some sang all away to school, but there were also big teasers. They liked to make fun of the rest of us. Sometimes we simply talked about the adventures we had had when were herding camels in different places.

We kept going home and back to school on our camels for about three months. Then our families had to move to another place far away from school for a few months before the big vacation, so we had to stay there at school during those months.

A problem was that we couldn't study during the night because therewas neither electricity nor much wood for fire. Luckily, the teacher had a petroleum lamp. It was very useful because it permitted him towork at night. After he finished his own work, he allowed us to carry the lamp to our hut. We placed the lamp on the sand and all huddled around it so we could memorize our lessons, because we had to recite our lessons in the classroom each morning. It was very difficultwith twenty-four students around one lamp. Sometimes the lamp ranout of petroleum, so we had to often wait for three days before it wasavailable again. There was only one car that would travel to the closest town for petroleum. Our teacher usually gave the driver a five-liter bottle to bring petroleum for him and for us as well.

During the times when we had no petroleum, we had to search for wood far away from our school to keep a fire going in the desert so we could study by fire light. As we studied, we were often disturbed by the smoke. By the end of the night, we all had red and sore eyes. It was very hard for me because I have only one eye. I usually had totake a break from the fires.

Another problem with our wood fire was that it attracted a lot of insects. That was because the area was not inhabited. Usually in thedesert when you light a fire, the flame attracts insects especially in the places where there are no people or animals. The flame even attracted scorpions sometimes. Scorpions bit two of my friends. Theywere badly stung. One of them became seriously sick. We saw him struggling to breathe. We thought he was going to die. Our teacher had no choice, so he sent him home because there was no doctor around. His parents had to take care of him by giving him traditional medicines from trees and pray for him.

After three years in this school, everyone began to leave because some of the families had to travel far away. Some students just gaveup. My mom decided to take me to another village far away from home again. This time it was nearly sixty kilometers from our camp in the Dannat area. This new school presented me with new challenges. I knew no one in the area, and there were many students from the city sent by their parents because they were distracted from their study by city life. The other students spoke Hausa, not Tuareg, which was a language I did not know. I foundmyself isolated and lonely. Once again, I tried unsuccessfully to escape from this school. It tookme two weeks to adjust and to begin to interact with other students. Ispent another three years in the second school. By high school, I was accustomed to school.

Physically getting to school was not easy. At the end of a big vacation when I was attending high school, I had to return to schoolfrom my village. My friend and I had waited for a week for the only transportation in the area, but, as had happened in the past, once again it never came. He had to get to work in Arlit and was afraid of losing his job. I had to go to Niamey where I was attending high school.

After the seventh day, we decided to walk to Arlit where he worked and lived and where I could catch the bus for the 1,300 km (800 mile) trip to the capital city. We had only a five-liter container of waterwith us when we set out at 8 AM into a dry and burning wind that was blowing down on us from the mountains. It was so blistering hotthat we had to stop frequently and take cover under a tree wheneverwe encountered one with shade. Whenever we saw a small tree wavering through the bubbling mirages of the desert, we would thinkit was a car. But, we never did see a single vehicle during the entire 16-hour trek.

We ran out of water before we got to Arlit. We did meet some peopleon their donkeys who were finished with their shopping in town and were heading to their home in the desert somewhere. They stopped and gave us some water. I didn't know them but they knew my grandfather. They didn't have cooked food with them, but they gave us a box of spaghetti and some sticks of matches to light a fire. We couldn't find anything to cook the meal in, so I decided to eat it as it was. It tasted so good that I thought there was sugar in it. When I told my friend, who had refrained from eating this delicacy, he smiledand made fun of me. "Hunger is the best sugar," he said.

When we finally arrived in Arlit it was midnight. I was supposed to take an old bus to Niamey, but they run infrequently as there are onlya few of them and I had to wait for another two days before I could leave on what is normally an 800 mile endurance test when all goeswell. On this trip nothing was destined to go well. The road between Arlit and Agadez is very bad. Its asphalt had been badly eroded andturned into pot-holes. The bus shook so hard that it felt like my intestines would get tangled up with my lungs. The final insult was delivered when at last we came into Agadez and were told that the normal road to Niamey was flooded. We had to take a loop passing through the south of Niger before we could head to Niamey. It was aslow and noisy two-day crawl during which we had to choose between choking on dust from open windows and the suffocating heat of closed ones. We finally limped into Niamey 12 days after our start. Such is transportation in Niger. We all know this and I acceptedit as the reality of our lives.

My mother had a strong belief. She has always told me that school isthe key to life nowadays. If you are not educated, you are consideredblind. Therefore, she was determined that I would receive an education. Later, I saw that educated people who had gone to schoolcould speak and read in different languages and were able to be successful in the modern world. Despite my difficult early experiences with "school," I now appreciate and value what my mother did for me by insisting on my education. Now I have possibilities that are not limited to herding camels in the Sahara Desert.

Drought

It was the beginning of the rainy season and not a drop of rain had yet fallen. The heat had become nearly unbearable, and a soul- sucking wind was continuously blowing. All our animals, our camels,our goats, our ewes and our donkeys, were growing thinner and thinner, and some were dying from the drought. We knew it was going to be a more challenging time than usual for our animals and for us as well. I had just returned home from school for my three months of summer vacation and now had to meet my responsibilitiesof taking care of the camels. My cousins and I were required to especially keep an eye on those camels already weakened by the drought and make sure they got to the well safely every two days. Before my return, a few camels had already died. It was painful formy people to see our camels weakening and then dying from the drought.

They were so precious to us. As my grandfather said, "Camels are our best friends and are related directly to our hearts." Ipersonally experienced the truth of this statement when, after my return, I saw four of our camels die in front of me.

I will never forget that experience. The first died as we were going to the well. I was leading one small group of camels when I realized that my cousin had fallen behind. As I led the camels forward, I heard him call out to me. "Ahmed, help me. We have to get him up." When I turned to look at him, I saw him behind the entire herd pacingaround a camel that was crouching on his haunches on the dry ground. When I reached them, I could see that the camel was nothing more than skin and bones. His thin front legs were folded in front of him and his rib bones protruded out at his sides like hard, thick cylinders curving around his mid-section. Beneath these bones lay sunken hollows in his back and stomach. My cousin and I stood on opposite sides of the camel and tried to reach under him with our hands to help him stand. I could feel the hard structure of his boney skeleton as we strained to raise him up, but his legs would not support him anymore and he kept folding in and down to the ground each time we tried to lift him. Next we slipped ropes under his belly and pulled them to once again help him rise. That's when we realized we were too late. We let go of the ropes, and he lowered hishead to the ground. Then with his eyes half closed, he began to puff out his final breaths. I will never forget the sound of life passing out of him. I witnessed the second death three days later as we were returning from the well. Some of the camels we were leading laid down on theground and rolled over on their backs to stretch out and rub their backs on the rough surface. When they stood back up, I noticed thatone seemed unable to raise himself. Again my cousin and I tried to lift him with our hands and arms. Once again, we were unable to support him. We moved on to the ropes, but were again unsuccessful. My cousin asked me to go ahead to our tents and tell my uncle that the camel named Abzao was crouching on the groundand was unable to get up. I ran to the tents, found my uncle and toldhim what was happening.

He gathered up some medicine from his father, my
grandfather, and put it in a pot. Then he rushed back toward
the well. I later learned that he arrived too late and that
Abzao had died before the medicine could be administered.

As time passed the camels weakened so much that two of
them were unable to even make it to the well. For several
days, we had to carry the water to them where they were
kneeling next to our tents. My grandfather was taking special
care of them by sharing our food and trying to feed them
medicines. He fed them ground millet and peanut leaves he
had bought in the town. They were able to survive for about
six days. Then one morning as we left our tent we saw oneof
them kneeling in the sand with her neck extended out from
her body. My grandfather stood beside her looking down at
her with sad eyes. There was nothing he could do. He knew
she was in her last moments, and indeed she died before we
could get ready to lead ourcamels to the well. When we
looked at her dead body, we both felt intense pain and
sadness. We had known this camel and had caredfor her
since we were small boys. We remembered her gentleness
and her loving nature. She would come to our tent first,
before the rest of the herd, each evening to be milked and
would greet us with her soft sniffs. She would then lean her
head in against ours so we could kiss her on her soft, furry
nose. Her name was Tawenakh, andI still remember the feel
of her muzzle.

The fourth camel died during the night while my grandfather
was caring for him. My grandfather had remained at his side
until he drewhis last breath. We discovered him the next
morning lying on his sidewith his long neck bent and his
head resting on the ground. Again, my grandfather grieved
for this lost member of our community. I will always
remember how my cousins and I had to drag his body off
away from our tents so we would not have to smell his
decaying carcass. It was a sad time for all of us and, as my
grandfather said, we still carry the presence of our dead
companions in our hearts.

Our situation was becoming more and more desperate. Our
very survival might be threatened. In order to save as many

of our camelsas possible, my grandfather decided we would have to lead them away to a site where the rains had begun to fall. Meanwhile the rest of the family would settle around the well closest to our tents with thegoats and ewes. As always, the entire family looked to my grandfather for guidance. Only he could determine where we would find that rainy area. He had a unique ability to interpret the most subtle signs of the natural world around us. When it was raining anywhere in that huge desert habitat, my grandfather could estimatewere the rain was falling just by listening to the roll and direction of the thunder and by watching the spears of lightning above the dunes.

That day, my cousin and I were climbing a tree to cut off some fresh branches for weak camels. As we hacked at the branches, we saw afew beautiful clouds above us, and we thought it was going to rain that day. Rolls of thunder groaned around us, but no rain fell. Nevertheless, my grandfather stood to the side of our tent motionless, lost in concentration. He was carefully noting the traces of thunder and lightning. When the clouds had finally disappeared, he turned and walked back to us to tell us what he had estimated theprobability of rain. He stood before those who had come to hear his words and said, "According to my estimation, this rain has shifted north with the heavy, black clouds. Therefore, the rain is now falling in the towns of Aghly or Arlit." These towns were fairly close to us somy cousins and I started laughing and dancing with joy and the hopeof saving our way of life.

The following morning my uncle Almahdi went to check out my grandfather's proclamation. My uncle told me later that when he reached the area around these towns, he could feel freshness of theair and smell the organic richness of wet ground. After examining thearea, however, he could see that it would take some weeks before the grass would be long enough for camels. The problem was that with the extremely hot weather, the water on the ground would evaporate quickly, and this process would prolong the growth. Luckily, my uncle knew that there was a small well in the area that hean his friends had dug when they used to travel to Algeria on camelsmany years before.

When my uncle got back to our camp, he gave us directions to theplace he had chosen. Fortunately, one of my cousins had once traveled to that area to look for one of our lost camels. He said he could find it, but he didn't know about the well.

It was agreed that my two cousins and I would set out across the desert in the early morning with the male camels. My uncle decidedto stay behind with the female camels to take special care of a pregnant camel that still hadn't delivered. He wanted to make sure she and her baby would have the best chance for survival. Therefore, my cousins and I left before our uncle. We knew he would be moving more slowly than us, and we wanted to make sure the male camels we were responsible for, and who were already suffering from the lack of water, could reach the designated area in time and have the best chance for survival.

We led the male camels from the backs of the camels we were riding. As we moved the males ahead, we could see that they wereseriously weakened from hunger and thirst. They were swaying slightly from side to side, and they lifted their legs slowly as if they were heavy weights. I carried our water in a goatskin hanging against the side of my camel with a small drinking bowl attached, while one of my cousins carried our food on his camel. As we traveled into the desert, we began to feel the effects of the drought. Despite the fact that we were protected by our turbans and tunics, itwas so scorching hot that we could feel our skin burning. The hard brittle wind drove against us and whistled in our ears like ghostly spirits. My cousins repeatedly shouted out to me to be careful with the water that I was carrying because it was the only water we had and we were not sure if we would even find any at our destination. Iknew I had a great responsibility. Water was life.

Although the pastureland we were heading toward was only a one-day journey from our home, it was a tedious, slow and exhausting

journey. The fierce, relentless wind continued to suck the moisture from our bodies as the day progressed. My single eye became sore and throbbed with pain, and when I looked at my companions, I could see that they were going through the same discomfort. They were all squinting tightly to protect their eyes which I could see werestreaked with red. My lips were dry and cracked like theirs, and the skin of their faces and arms was parched and spotted like mine. Wewere all fighting to conserve our energy and to force ourselves through the fiery atmosphere. The camels that carried us began to sway slightly from side to side as their weakened legs began to fold.I could sense the fear that had gripped my cousins and was flowing into all the camels we were leading. I, myself, had to push down a rising sense of anxiety that I might collapse with my camel and allowthe water to escape from the goatskin. While we moved along, I would occasionally pour a bowl of water from the skin for both meand the cousins to help us maintain some level of strength and direction.

As the afternoon passed, the sun began to lower in the west. By then, we were so drained and weakened that we were moving in adream-like state, dazed and confused. Nevertheless, we knew wehad to press forward or we all would die from dehydration.

We were traveling now through a series of low dunes interspersed with black rocks, some of which were almost buried in the driving sand. I noted that the few small trees we passed had totally dried to a dull, dark reddish hue. None of them had any leaves or any sign oflife or promise of foliage. Even their bark had been stripped away bythe power of the wind. The wind had even torn some of them out by the roots, and they now lay in the sand like huge black spiders with long spindly legs reaching upwards into the sky. As we passed a small cave in one of the rocks, two gazelles sprang out and raced across the desert before us. For a moment, they paused and turned their heads to look back at us over their shoulders, their hides goldenbrown against the fading light of the afternoon. Then they turned again and danced gracefully away across the sand. I watched them move off with a sense of awe and longing, which soon turned to a sense of despair. They seemed to be the only life left in this desiccated land.

As we fought to push forward, it seemed like our journey would never end. It seemed as if we were moving into an unnatural world ofdevastating wind and heat. None of us could any longer speak because our mouths had been drained of all moisture and our dry tongues had become lumps of hard flesh. We continued to look ahead into the deepening darkness with only one thought echoing in our heads, "Go, go, go."

Finally, my cousin motioned to us that we had reached our camping site. I noticed a change in the air. The extreme dryness was beginning to yield to a slight suggestion of moisture. I also noticed that my camel had lowered his head to the surface mud to feed on the sparse grasses that were beginning to grow there. I still held the rope that was secured to his nose, and as his head moved forward and down, my upper body slid forward with it, and I had to reach back with one hand to grab the camel's hump to catch myself before I fell. Nevertheless, I felt a deep sense of hope and relief. Next we allcaught sight of an acacia tree my uncle had used as a marker for us by tying a piece of his old white turban to the top branches. We couldsee it in the moonlight. Yes, we had arrived.

It was now the middle of the night. As we climbed down from our camels, I was so tired that I even forgot to remove the rope in my camel's nose. Not one of us bothered to lay his rug on the ground.We just collapsed on the sand and lay there motionless like dead bodies.

When we woke up in the morning we could see our animals feeding on the low grass, and it was a beautiful sight. We only had pounded millet and some rice with us, and we had to go look for wood in orderto cook. We stored our saddles and supplies under a small tree and settled in to wait for our uncle. By the middle of the day, we had finished our last water and were becoming anxious for our uncle to arrive and show us the location of the well. It had been almost a fatal error to have engaged this journey without knowing where we couldfind water when we arrived at our destination.

With our water gone, my older cousin suggested that we should check around to see if we might discover some stagnant water insidethe rocks. We began to explore the area around the camp, walking out to check the rocks that surrounded us. That was when I realized my mouth and throat were so dry I was not able to speak anymore. Whenever I tried to form a word, I could feel the dry, hot wind sucking the last bits of moisture from my mouth. I wondered if I would ever be able to speak again. Although we did not discover anystagnant pools, we could see some scattered spots where water hadevaporated. If a spot still felt damp, we would lie down on that spot for a moment hoping to absorb even a single drop of moisture.

Eventually, we decided to hike back to our camp and to try to be patient. We were now very worried about our uncle. We had hoped that the camel had given birth by then and that my uncle only had towait for only a brief time for the baby to be able to walk.

It was almost sunset, and we were all craving even a tiny drop of water. We were able to sleep that night, but we were thirsty to thepoint that we knew we were in trouble. In the morning, I could see that each of the my cousins' eyes had sunken inside their heads. As it was getting hotter and hotter through the day, I started feeling a terrible exhaustion sweeping through me. My older cousin was feeling a little bit better than the younger cousin and me, because hewas more experienced than we were. My biggest problem was that whenever I tried to get up I became dizzy and tended to faint and falldown. There was also a disturbing noise rumbling in my ears. I had ahard time breathing and sometimes my breath escaped through my ears whenever I tried to swallow.

My older cousin tried to draw some camel urine for us, but he couldnot draw a single drop. I wanted to cry, and I tried. The emotions were real, but there were no tears, so I cried tearlessly for the first time in my life. My voice became thin and barely audible as I shookwith sobs. We all had severe headaches. I wanted to urinate, and although I could hardly walk and had to keep pushing my body up from the ground as I moved, I managed to make my way a short distance from our camp to relieve myself. The passing of urine was surprisingly painful and there was only a small amount that trickled out. I reeled and stumbled as I returned to my cousins. When I laid down beside them, I could hardly recognize them. Everything in myline of vision was blurred. I rested my head in the sand and, lookingup at the sky, and started to see hallucinations whenever I blinked. Bursts of color pulsated in front of my eyes. I felt like the muscles surrounding my one remaining eye were collapsing and feared I would lose it. I was also struggling to protect the socket of my lost eye from the swirling sand by raising my hand to cover it. Everything was becoming dim and distorted for me. At the same time, our older cousin was making fun of my younger cousin and me and teasing us, "What's up? Should I bury you guys. Just let me know whenever you are ready." We tried to flash a slight smile at him and then turnedaway from his jeers as we lay there on the ground.

On the third morning, as we huddled close to one another in the morning light, my older cousin suddenly heard the sounds of the female camels nearing us. "Look," he said to us raising his hand to point in the direction we had traveled. As we followed his signal, wecould see our uncle in his white turban approaching on his camel. The tails of the turban were flapping lightly in the warm wind. He had left the other female camels behind him to feed on the grasses in thevalley. When he neared us, we could see that he was carrying waterin his goatskin. He jumped down from his camel holding the goatskincontainer before him. He passed it from one of us to the next, raisingthe container above each of our heads and one by one he poured water on each of us. It felt so good when he poured it on me I eventried to catch the drops with my mouth. However, he gave us only alittle bit to drink, because if we drank too much water he knew we would vomit. I could feel a soothing coolness running through my whole body. Once again I could focus my vision and see properly. My uncle and my older cousin decided they would travel to the wellmy uncle knew was somewhere nearby and left us to cook lunch with the water that he had brought. Even when I was not thirsty anymore, I tried to get up but found I couldn't yet walk properly.Nevertheless, our crisis was over. We were saved.

Water

We have a saying, "Aman Iman, koutilan aman yille atama" which means "water is life and as long as there is water, there is hope fordesert inhabitants." The same words are written in Tifinagh, our alphabet. I spent all my childhood and energy looking for water andpasture in the desert. In the desert, sometimes we don't have a drink for up to two full daysbecause there is no water and we have to walk or ride camels for a distance of up to twenty-three kilometers to find a well. Sometimes the well is empty or you may have to wait for hours until the well replenishes and the water deepens. When water finally comes as rain, it is always welcome, but it canalso be destructive.

In the rainy season, sometimes there are floods. They can carry weak animals away. There are not enough trees behind which to take refuge. One year, there was a terrible flood in our area, and itswept away my uncle Ghissa's entire herd of goats and ewes. People called that place "Ghissa's Tragedy." He was left with nothingexcept his hunting dog. His relatives decided to give him a couple of goats and ewes so he could begin again. We spent that entire rainy season shocked about that tragedy.

Big trucks come from the nearest towns to carry firewood back from the desert for the town dwellers. They cut down the few trees to sell them in the town. My grandfather is and has always been against this abuse. His approach, even now, is to try to convince them to findtheir firewood in the south where there is a forest. As a leader of the herders within my community, he is respected and listened to. He is known to be knowledgeable in many natural and traditional facts.

The heavy trucks turn the ground into pounded dirt with their tires. They erase the pasture wherever they pass. Sometimes they run down camels or donkeys. The people who drive the trucks also maycause bushfires because they don't pay attention to where they throw their cigarettes. One time there was a huge bushfire where welived during the cold season that was caused by the truck people. Three families lost their tents as well as their food supply in that tragedy. Fortunately, there were no humans lost because the fire wasignited at a time when no one was at home. As usual in the morning,people had left their tents to deal with animals and greet neighbors.

During the rainy season people use the murky water that flows fromcreeks and catch terrible diseases from the dirty creek water. According to the elders, these diseases are mostly caused by the rotting of animal corpses. Once my family lost eighteen head of ewesand sixteen goats. The dry season lasts so long that the animals become very weak and hungry. When the rain comes, hundreds of animals die because they can't resist the cold and the wetness on their skins. Another problem during the rainy season occurs when the ground gets wet. As they graze, animals sometimes are drawn into quicksand and die miserably struggling to escape the force thatpulls them to their deaths. When animals die, they remain in the desert. Rainwater that falls on their decaying bodies enters runningwater and also seeps into the sand and, ultimately, down into the wells beneath.

In the desert, animals represent our unique wealth. In some families,some particular animals are considered members of the family. It is really painful to see your animals being carried away by water and there is nothing that can be done to save them.

Extended Family

In the Niger desert, there is always time for community and for the sharing of our lives. We depend on one another for survival, and weknow this. Therefore our families and our communities are vitality important to us. As our saying goes, "Sinimigagat yananawan taznamahazm iwalanwan," which means "set up your tents a little bit farther apart,but keep your hearts closer." It's very important to visit your neighbors' houses every morning or whenever you can. People constantly check whether their neighbors are doing well or whether they might need something. In the desert people live as a community. They do everything together. For instance, if you run out of salt or tea,you can send a child to get some from the neighbors. Sometimes, if someone needs to harvest his garden, he will ask his neighbors to come to help him. The only thing he will do in return is make a huge meal that day for everybody.

The same thing happens when a well is needed. The elders have to decide first where it is going to be dug. It takes sometimes two to five days to make that decision. The elders travel around the area examining the trees, the surface of the sand and other signs that only they understand. After that, the young men gather and start digging the well. At lunchtime, each house brings lunch for these workers. Forthe young men, it's shameful not to be a member of the well diggers. Digging wells is part of the honor code of our people. If, however, you are among the older members of the community, you are not expected to do the hard, manual work, but only to offer ideas and guidance.

In the desert, the tent is considered a haven for all travelers, and the wife is responsible for taking care of guests. People are constantly traveling between different pasturelands. Sometimes they travel fromanother part of the region to seek their lost camels or goats. The length of the journey depends on where the person first heard news of his missing animals. Often it takes three to five days to get back home again after trying to find lost camels. Before the traveler beginshis search, he has to make sure he brings enough food and water with him to face his journey. As the saying goes, "tisena dagh teklenak wirtissena dagh tewaghlenak," which means "you know about your departure, but you never know about your return day." In reality, the search is usually a great opportunity to travel between different areas of the desert. The traveler has a chance to see someplaces that may be better than where he is from because of the availability of pasture or water. Sometimes the trip permits the traveler to see many of his relatives and friends during his journey.

The best part of being in the desert is that you don't really have toknow people in order to spend the night or the day with them. As I mentioned, the tent is a haven for travelers. That's why wherever yousee a tent, you can stop there to pass the night or the day. If it's during the night, you see the wood-fire and just head towards it. All you have to say once you get there is,"Assalamu ahleikoum," which is a religious expression in Arabic that means, "peace be upon you."It's an Islamic greeting. In response, the man of the tent will come tohis guest to welcome him under a tree. He will make sure that the guest feels as if he were at home. The host's children will come to tend the guest's camel. Some children will get blankets and water.The first thing to bring to the guest is water, because you never know whether he might have run out of water a few days before he arrived at the tent. Once the visitor is settled, the man of the house will send one of his children to other neighbors to announce that his father has a guest. They will all send cooked food for their neighbor's guest and, of course, they will come to greet him. When the guest has relaxed from the long and endless journey on thesea of sand, it's time for "Ezabaz N salan" which means "getting some news from the guest." It's generally the news of his people and the pastureland he has passed through. Then after dinner, everybody in the neighborhood will come to greet and talk with the guest again. We Tuareg also have a custom we call "Essembagh n temet" which means "to try to discover if the guest is related to you." It's usually the job of the elders to do that. When the guest is ready to leave, the manof the house will make sure that he has everything he needs with him,such as food and water. In the desert, people tend to move slowly and to reserve time for one another. We value community and make our relationships an important part of our everyday lives.

I can remember one time after dinner. Night was falling in the desert.The shadows of the dunes were growing longer and spreading out across the sand. The glowing sun was sinking down towards the horizon. All of the neighbors in our camp flooded to my grandfather'stent. They gathered outside on blankets laid out upon the sand

and quietly traded stories, stories about the past, stories about French colonization, stories about "ashak," the honor code of the Tuareg people. "Respect all peoples, especially women." "As a man, you must help your elders when you find them doing hard work." "Don't bring shame upon yourself, because the desirable women will hear about it." "Don't ever lie." "Better to break your leg than to break yourword."

They also talked about how to care for their camels. "You must trainyour camel to move gracefully in the desert." After that exchange, they began to tease and challenge one another about how each might react in a difficult situation. "What would you do if a camel fellwith you on its back and you also fell to the ground and the tie gathering your pants broke? What if you grabbed at only your shirt when you got up and you lost your pants? Hmmmmmmm. Big embarrassment."

Everyone enjoyed this time of shared conversation at the end of a day in the desert, and the neighbors continued to challenge one another. "What if you were standing around the well with your wife and mother-in-law and you were washing clothes? What if you wereonly wearing your wife's scarf to hide yourself and as you took the water from the well, you slipped and dove towards the well and your wife wanted to grab your leg to help you? Should she call her motherto help? What would her mother see if the scarf slid down with you? Should your wife let you go down rather than risk exposing you by grabbing one leg?" There were different responses. Some suggestedthat the wife let him go rather than disrespect the mother-in-law by exposing her to an unwelcome sight. Others suggested that the wife throw wet sand up onto the husband to hide what should be private. There was quiet laughter.

Then everyone looked up and focused on my grandfather, the poet and historian of our people. He had just finished his evening prayers while sitting on his rug on the east side of his tent as he did every dayat sunset. Now he was walking toward us, ready, as always, to share his observations and his memories with my people.

He reached his folding bed which was placed on the west side of histent and sat down in the dim light of a half moon. As usual, he was dressed in his black tunic and pants. On his head he wore his black turban. As he often did, he picked up a small child and held him gently on his lap. Then he began to ask us what we had done during the day and reminded us young boys of our responsibilities in tendingthe small camels. Next he moved on to share with us how things were in the past when there were many more animals in the desert surrounding my tribe, both domesticated goats and camels and wildantelope, sheep and addax.

As he spoke about that past, I realized how different that past was from our present. I thought of the recent climate changes we were experiencing because of the expanding desertification of the Sahara.It was one of my grandfather's greatest concerns and sorrows. He knew how threatening this change could be for my people, how it could destroy their way of life, how it could, in fact, destroy them. When I heard him talk about the past, I often felt a longing to return towhat was and I would try to call up images of a more supportive environment for my people.

My grandfather also reminded us about the days of French colonization and the great suffering the French had brought to our people. He spoke of how the French forced the Tuaregs to do highlydemanding, difficult and even life-threatening work, such as buildingroads through the desert in the intense heat of the dry season. Further, he spoke about the huge taxes the French levied on theanimals of the Tuareg tribe. How could this be possible?

Another great concern of my grandfather was the mining of our natural resources by the French. In the soft light of the wood fire before his tent, I could see the sadness in his eyes as he spoke aboutthe way in which the French used my people to search for archaeological specimens in the mountains and used these specimens to build their own wealth, sharing nothing with the Tuaregs. Finally, he talked about the Kaocen and Rhabidine Revolution when Tuaregs rebelled against French occupation. They fought with all of their strength and their courage to defend their land. But they were up against impossible odds. The French were heavily armed with a great variety of small and large guns and artillery. The native population had to face this modern armed force with only the swordsand spears they had fashioned themselves and a scattering of ratherprimitive muzzleloaders they had captured in their past history from previous invaders. Ultimately Kaocen himself was killed by the Italians somewhere in Libya as he continued to travel the desert to defend and support his people.

As often happens, that night, as we listened to my grandfather, Tuaregs from as far away as the south of Algeria had joined us to askhim about their heritage, about how they were related to another Tuareg tribe in Niger. It is my grandfather who preserves our oral traditions. He is the source of our knowledge and understanding of our own past. He is famous throughout the Sahara as a wise man and a conservator of our history.

When we were young, my cousins and I were always very close to our grandfather. He was not only the wise man of the village, but alsothe poet and singer. He would sing his poems accompanied by the violin which was always played by a designated woman of the tribe. He tried many times to teach us some of his poetry, but we couldn't ever seem to master it. Only one of my youngest cousins, Kununu, was able to learn many of my grandfather's poems, poems Kununu could also sing. One beautiful morning, I was sitting under a tree down by the creekbed behind our tent with my younger brother and my grandfather. I was making tea for my grandfather and listening to him tell some amazing stories about "ashak," the honor code of the Tuareg. He shared this rich tradition of my people with the two of us.

He said, when he was younger, one night he went to sing his poetrywith the lady who was playing the Inzad at that time. The Inzad, is very important in Tuareg society. My mother plays the Inzad. It is aninstrument made up of only one string and is played with a bow. It is used for both therapeutic and recreational purposes. The therapeuticpurpose of the Inzad is to accompany the song of a poet in order to drive evil spirits away. It is believed that when the Inzad is played, thepeople become so joyous that evil spirits run in fear.

Recreationally, the Inzad accompanies a poem sung by a poet to celebrate the bravery and heroism of warriors. In the past, when theTuaregs were waging wars against colonial troops, the Inzad playedan important role in encouraging the warriors to be brave and courageous in battle. The Inzad is usually played where young menand young ladies meet together at night. The rule is that no matter what happens to you during "Inzad," you can't move nor can you takeoff your turban. Everyone must try to be as elegant and respectful as possible.

One night, my grandfather traveled with two of his friends on their camels to the tent in which the lady who was playing the violin thatnight lived. As they were riding their camels, they saw a wood fire where the "Inzad" would be held. When they reached that site, everybody stood to greet the great poet and singer. Then the partybegan. After my grandfather had been singing for a short time to the melodyof the Inzad, he stopped singing and whispered to those close to him that he felt something like a rope sneaking through his pants. Of course, he showed no fear. For a Tuareg male, it's shameful to be afraid of anything in front of women. As he resumed his singing, he slowly reached up his pant leg to check what was moving about inside. Then, suddenly, his fingers located the source of his discomfort as he felt a long, slithering body climbing up his leg. Heknew it was a huge snake.

Still unwilling to show fear, he kept singing while, at the same time, hewas now moving his hand up the outside of his pant leg searching for the head of the snake. When he located the head, he used his powerful hand to smash it. No one was aware of what had happened as everybody was enjoying the party, some even screaming with joy. Next, my grandfather slowly slid his hand into the pant leg, grabbed the tail of the snake and threw it away without being seen. When the party was over, he told the lady who had played the violin that he had just managed to secure some meat for her and that she wouldreceive it in the morning.

I remember another night when my cousins and I were lying close to my grandfather in the sand. He was reclining on his small prayer rug, and suddenly he smiled and looked directly at me. He asked me if I had any poem that I would like to share. Unfortunately, I was not really interested in poetry at that time. I stared up at the stars and toldhim that I was trying to think of one, but all I could think about was how to break my young camel in properly and how to realize my dream of finding water close to where we lived. Everyone laughed at me, because I was not able to think of anything that had to do with poetry. Was I really my grandfather's grandson?

My grandfather is not only important among my people, but he is alsovery much loved, honored and appreciated by all the camels of the family. He has much knowledge about camel diseases. Many people in the area bring their sick camels to my grandfather.

I remember when one of our neighbors led his camel to my grandfather's tent. We all immediately knew what was wrong. The camel was walking with its head near, and almost scraping, the ground. It could not raise its neck. My grandfather walked up to the sick camel and stretched out his hands to feel the camel's neck. He then announced to us that there was only cold blood in the neck. Noblood was circulating.

Next, he used both hands to open the camel's mouth so that he couldpeer inside. After this examination, he called to my cousin to bring him his leather bag in which he carried all of his special supplies, including his tools. After my cousin handed him the bag, my grandfather pulled from it a tool shaped like a screwdriver with awooden handle. As three men held the camel securely, my grandfather jabbed this sharp tool into the camel's paw and allowedthe camel's blood to flow for a moment into the sand. We all heard the bellow of the camel as it echoed over the sand. Then, my grandfather applied a mixture of herbs from his bag to the open wound to stop the bleeding.Then he pulled out a larger tool that had a long, curved blade. He putthis tool into the fire to heat it until it shone red. With this tool, he walked to the rear of the camel and placed the heated tool againstthe camel's flesh above its tail. The camel bellowed again as my grandfather removed his blade. The next step he took was to mix some pounded millet with water anda traditional medicine. He is the only one in my tribe that knows what this traditional medicine contains. He then placed the mixture into a pot. Having prepared this balm, my grandfather returned to the head of the camel and once again forced its mouth open, holding the camel's tongue securely so the animal would not choke. Then he poured the mixture down the camel's throat. The camel coughed and sputtered. We all stood there watching the scene as my grandfather assured everyone present that the camel would be fine. Based on his words, we all knew the camel would be. My grandfather's curative powers were so well trusted that we all had total faith in his skills and his judgment.

My grandfather not only has the ability to heal our camels. He alsohas a profound power to communicate with them. They sense the presence of his spirit. There are some milk camels in our herd thatwon't accept anyone milking them except my grandfather. Sometimes my grandfather will go to visit some relatives far away inthe desert. It can often take him up to two to three days to get back home. Every two months, it is his custom to ride his camel to visit allof his family members and friends as well. It's something that we Tuareg people call,"Alhakh N'tamette," which stands for "your duty towards relatives." During that time, while my grandfather is away, ithas always been impossible to approach three specific camels that belong to members of our family. The camels will kick anyone who dared come close to them.

One evening, when my grandfather was still away and we had already tied up the small camels for the night, their mothers started arriving back to our camp. My aunt decided to dress up like my grandfather so she could try to milk these specific three camels. She wore my grandfather's black tunic and his long black turban. I was standing just behind her holding the wooden bowl which we use to catch the milk from the camel's breasts. My aunt had fashioned the turban in the same way her father fashioned it. As she was walking up to one of these camels, she made a noise that we make to calm the camels while approaching them. Unfortunately the camel alreadyknew that "man" was not my grandfather. My aunt is a short woman, and she doesn't really look like my grandfather. As we watched her, we were laughing at her because she reminded us of someone that everyone knew in the village, someone we loved who used to teach children the Koran. My mother shouted in laughter to my aunt, "Don't go closer to that camel. She will kick you."

Ignoring the warning, my aunt moved closer and tried to reach the teats of the camel to milk it while I was standing behind her getting ready to hold the bowl properly. Out of the side of my eye, I suddenlysaw the tails of the unraveling turban flying through the air. I immediately knew what had happened. My mother's warning had come true. The camel had kicked. I moved quickly away from the camel and, looking back, saw my aunt lying on the sand, shaking withlaughter. The kick was painful, but she couldn't stop laughing at the character she had created in her own dress-up performance.

My grandfather's biggest fear now is the uranium mining in the region. A French company has been mining since 1974 in Arlit, whichis the nearest town to where my people herd their animals. That areaused to be a pastureland for my people. My grandfather told me that he used to herd his camels in the exact location where the company had set up their clinic. Recently, the same company decided to extend its search for new uranium mines in the area. They have discovered a new mining site in the middle of our pastureland. Canadian and Chinese companies are also beginning a search forthe same resources. My grandfather's worst fears seem to be our reality. I also share his fear and his concern for my people.

One day I was sitting under a tree with my grandfather and Mouhamed one of his cousins. My grandfather suddenly fell silent for a moment and, wiping his tears away with his black turban, said to me, "I'm just wondering where those companies want us to go!" He told me, "This is our land. I don't know where else we would go if those companies continue occupying our pasture." Mouhamed, his cousin, quietly confessed that the worst part of what was happening was that these companies are not even willing to dig wells for our people. It seems that they have no concern for, nor desire to help, theTuaregs.

Everyone in the family sees my grandfather as a role model, and everyone wants to be like him. We enjoyed being with our grandfather so much that sometimes we used to ask him if we could sleep in his bed. He taught us many lessons about life and how to be kind, gentle and compassionate with others. He is a very peaceful and tolerant human being. He has always insisted that all members ofthe family maintain and protect their internal peacefulness for only if the soul is peaceful can we enjoy life.

My grandfather was deeply inspired by the silence and the emptinessof the desert. He used to say to us, "God created countries with muchwater for men to live in and He created deserts for men to discover their souls." He motivated us to meditate on that proverb. As we pondered the meaning of the proverb, we too began to understand that the spirit of the desert was the primary force that shaped the values, beliefs and sense of belonging of my people.

I learned a great deal from this inspired and inspiring man about how to behave as a human being, how to respect and value others while, at the same time, respecting and being true to oneself. I carry and willalways carry these beautiful and instructive memories with me. They have formed and shaped my life. My grandfather believes that violence and war are caused by our human failure to understand and respect others. He said, "If someone hurts you, try to write down that pain on the sand so that the wind will blow it away, and if someone does something good to you, try to write it on a rock so that the wind will never erase it."

PART 2.
a Nomad in America

A Different Kind of Desert

When I first arrived in America, there were many surprises.

In New Hampshire, I remember thinking there was an unbelievableamount of water! It was like a dream to me. The only thing I had in mind was "Why does this injustice exist?" Many people were complaining about rain. They didn't want much rain while we, in theSahara, are dying from the lack of rain. To my amazement, I found that people used lakes just for fun. They rode around in their boats on the lakes or fished. They didn't even use these fish for food, butjust as recreation. When I came to Scottsdale, Arizona I was newly surprised by the man-made created environment. I was told that the southwest was ina multi-year critical drought, but I could not make sense of that. Everywhere I looked, I saw fountains and sprinklers spewing watereverywhere. It was very beautiful to watch, but it made me remember my thirst at home as a boy. That is why I felt pain in my heart.

My host family and their friends told me that we were living in a desert. While the temperature in Scottsdale sometimes felt familiar, nothing else suggested to me anything resembling the desert I had known. Even to say, as some suggested, that Scottsdale is more likean extended oasis is to greatly understate the overwhelming differences, oases and all. In fact, I felt I was living not in a different desert, but on a different planet, a planet paradise with one startling surprise after another.

I thought, "I wish our desert were like this kind of desert." Then I asked myself how I could make this happen in the Niger desert. Theonly response I received was "After the judgment day maybe." Afterpondering the differences, I tried to analyze the differences. I figuredout that Americans have already passed the stage of struggling to find water. They are designing sprinklers and fountains for decoration and to create beauty around them. That is because they have been able to harness technology and engineering to find, channel, capture, use and recycle water in a purposeful manner.

I realized that by applying knowledge, skill and resources that a harsh, desert environment had been made accommodating to life. Itmade me think that perhaps I could help make changes to support my own people. I don't want to construct golf courses or artificial lakes and fountains. I just want to help my people survive with basic resources such as wells and areas for gardening. I want to help themfight back against the already progressing desertification of the land.

Another difference is we don't have air conditioners in the Niger desert. A group that gets a chance to settle near a nice shade tree isthe lucky one. It's our air conditioner and we spend most of the day under it drinking green tea. Some tell stories and others tease each other in a harmonious atmosphere. This important sharing creates asense of togetherness. I realize that we may never acquire the luxuries of Scottsdale and in some ways that may be a good thing.

I am fascinated by the many differences between my world and the world I have been exposed to in the United States. I would never have guessed that some are able to play golf on a huge golf coursethat looks like an oasis. If the golf course were in the Niger desert, itwould have been used to feed animals. So much grass could serve for a whole season. My people would feel blessed by such abundance, but I wonder what is traded off in this contrast of cultures.

Automobiles

The first time I watched traffic in the United States, I ask myself the question, "Where are all these people going in their sleek and shiny cars?" They hurried by me in all types of cars, in cars of all different sizes, shapes and colors. I often traveled by bus in Scottsdale and spent a great deal of time waiting at bus stops. That was when I wasmost filled with amazement as vehicles rushed by me. They reminded me of swarms of ants skittering across the concrete surface of the roads. Even when I listened to music on earphones firmly in my ears, I often couldn't hear what was playing because theroar of engines and the swish of tires blotted out all other sounds. The cars raced by me, one car chasing the one in front of it as if they are connected by invisible wires. I wondered what it would be like if Iwere looking down on these roadways from the sky. Could I then seewhere they were headed? Or would I just see these lines of cars, these tiny insects, rushing along a complex network of concrete roadways? What a different world the United States is. Noise, speed, tires sizzing along the pavement, the loud swish of air as they pass. How different from our camel traffic in Niger. I thought about the calm andrelative silence of the movement across our desert. What did we hear? The soft plodding of camel hoofs in the muffling sand. No roar.No whoosh. No congestion. Only the sound of the breezes and the birds flying overhead. Sometimes only the ring of silence in our ears.

When I was a boy living in the desert, I used to spend as many as six months without seeing even one car, and if I saw one, I used to be frightened of it. I always thought it was going to knock me down if I came close to it. I didn't understand that cars were actually controlled by drivers. I thought they moved on their own. I also didn't know that cars burned gas. I believed they drank water like people or camels.

I remember one day when I was only seven years old. Two of my young cousins and I were helping my older sister build a fence to contain our herd of goats. Caring for the goats was her responsibilityas a young girl in our tribe. My sister had carried an armful of sticks from a lightly treed area near our camp and had stacked them on theground as we stood behind my grandmother's tent.

It was during the cold season, and during that season, many tourists would come to visit us, to take pictures of my people and our animals, of our clothing and our ceremonies. The Tuareg drivers whobrought these tourists to our camp, often requested that we perform a special dance or a camel race for the visitors. During these races, the men would mount their camels and drive them forward and the women would play the drums. The tourists loved to watch the camelsrunning around in a large circle, kicking up the sand, with turbaned riders on their backs. They also loved the rhythmic beat of the drums. We were always excited to see the cars full of tourists arrivebecause they would bring us gifts, clothing, pens and pencils, and, what we children loved most, candy. We also loved the new smell they brought with them. We loved to sniff the smell of fuel burning. There are few smells in the dryness of the desert, and we were fascinated by this exotic "fragrance."

That day, as we picked up the sticks one by one to fashion them intoa round fence for the goats, we looked up and saw a huge swirl of dirt moving toward us. At the same time, we heard the strange purring sound of an engine, a purr which grew louder as an automobile approached. When it reached us, we saw that the driver was one of my older cousins. He was also a desert guide who had brought a group of tourists from the city of Agadez. As the huge blue station wagon pulled into our camp, we stood stillout of respect for our visitors. In truth, we stood still because we were frozen in fear of the huge blue beast that had arrived. My cousin parked the car on the east side of the tent, and the tourists climbed out. As they looked around at their new environment, my uncle approached and greeted them. We children turned back and continued to build our fence, but we kept an eye on that threatening vehicle. This group of tourists had brought small tents with them and camped with us for three days waiting for another car from Agadez to catch up with them.

One morning, during their stay, I was sitting around a fire with my aunt and a cousin in front of my aunt's tent. The cousin and I had milked a goat who had given birth three days before. Now, we were cooking the milk in a metal pan, hardening it into cheese. My cousin,who was the driver, walked out of his uncle's tent to the car which was parked nearby. When he reached the vehicle, he called to me to bring him some water in a big teapot. I filled the teapot from the goatskin hanging on the side of our tent and, trying to control the fearthat was rising in my throat, carried it to him where he stood next to the car. Then I stepped back to watch him as he reached inside the open window of the car and pulled on something I could not see. Suddenlythe front of the car popped open with a loud snap. I jumped in reaction to the sound and stared at the broad narrow "smile" that hadopened along the front of the vehicle. It seemed to me as if it were a mouth. My cousin then reached under the upper lip of that "mouth" and lifted it up with both hands. It opened widely. Next he pulled up an iron bar and hooked it into the roof of what I later learned was called the hood. I began backing away from this huge gaping "mouth" as my cousin took the teapot from my hands. Now I knew Iwould find out if what I believed was, in fact, true. Did cars drink water? My cousin lifted the pot and emptied the water into its wide-open mouth and then disconnected the rod and slammed the top down. Then I knew my theory was proven. Now I was sure. Cars really do drink water.

I had another experience with this water-drinking machine. I was withmy uncle and his cousin, Mohammed, who owned a car. He had come to visit us from the city and had parked his car under a huge tree. We were all sitting under the tree together when we saw a friend of my uncle moving toward us through the desert on his camel. They were moving at a fast pace, kicking up large clouds of sand, and seemed to be in a great rush. We knew he was coming from far away, which surprised us.

When he rode the camel into camp, he headed toward the tree we sat around as he slowed his camel to a stop. He quickly climbed down to greet us. In response, everyone stood to welcome him with respect, and my uncle greeted him in Tuareg, "Awoud amadal tezekit azman," which means "please take a seat." If a visitor does not sit when he arrives, it means that something is wrong or he's in trouble.This visitor did not sit. Instead he remained standing and waved withhis hands that he could not sit. We knew then that he was in trouble.His face was tense and lined with worry as he explained to us that he was on an urgent mission and could not stay to visit. He had come searching for a car to bring his sick wife to the hospital and had heard that he might find one in our camp.I knew he had come in search of Mohammed's car which glinted in the sunlight on the other side of the tree. At first, I felt relieved. We could help him. We could help save his wife. But to my surprise, I saw Mohammed walk up to him with his hands extended and a look of concern in his eyes as he said to him something about "oil de moteur" which means "engine's oil." What he was saying was that he didn't have engine oil in his car, so he could not drive it until he couldsend to the town for more oil. This was upsetting news for our visitor.He had traveled a great distance and had not been able to help his wife. He knew he would have to return home and carry her by camelto the hospital which might take several more days. With a look of grief and worry lining his face, he climbed back on his camel and together they turned away from us to re-cross the desert.

Now as I watched him go, in my head I had formed an idea. "Oil de moteour" sounded to me exactly like "aowal de moteur" that means in my language (Tamasheq) "engine's heart," because the name "oil" sounds like "aowal" which means heart. I kept quiet about my confusion until we walked from the tree back to my uncle's tent to retrieve the meal which we would carry back with us to eat under the tree. As we entered the tent, I looked up at him and asked him the question that was haunting me. "Do cars have hearts like people?" He looked down at me and smiled for a moment, but he finally answered my question. "Ahmed, I know almost nothing about cars, nor anything about the French language, nor about any westerners' creations. However, I do know that cars don't have hearts and what you heard was 'oil de moteur.' It's a liquid for the engine. The only two things I do know about cars, are when they are ready to go I know how to get in and go and when they need to be pushed in order to get them started, I know how to push them."

In the United States, cars surrounded me almost everywhere I went.Everyone owns at least one car and sometimes even two. When I see them rush by me, I no longer think that they drink water or havehearts. However, I do know that they are an essential part of American life. In fact, they may indeed represent the beating heart of American culture.

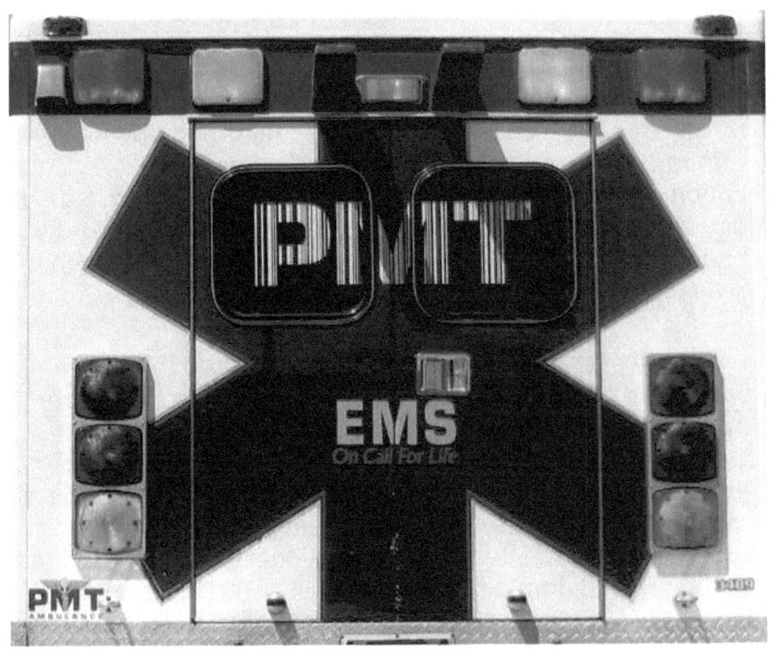

Medical Services

One morning while living in Scottsdale, I had gotten up later thannormal and had just prepared my favorite breakfast of Cheerios, bananas and milk. Before sitting down I tuned my host family's iPhone to a French language station in Niger so that I could hear news from home. Before I could even find the station, the quiet of our dead-end street was shattered by the wailing of an enormous yellow fire engine the size of a Niger bus passing within a few feet of the front window.

I had never even seen a fire engine before, except in a magazine one time, and here was one almost rattling the windows. I shivered a little as I ran to see what was happening, but I can't tell you whetherit was from fear, surprise or excitement. What was wrong? I had never heard such a sound before.

Before I could even get to a window, a second vehicle screaming a similar sound raced by the front of the house. It was red, not quite aslarge, a vehicle unfamiliar to me. Once I got a better look I saw that ithad PMT written on its side in big, white letters above the word ambulance. It's a word that I had never heard before and I wonderedwhy it was with a fire engine, which I knew was for putting out fires.

I became even more confused when I noticed that there was no smoke anywhere near to where the two vehicles had stopped in frontof the house next door. A number of large, strong looking men were jumping out of the sides of these trucks and sprinting toward that house. After a few minutes two men, dressed in matching dark blueuniforms with those same letters PMT on the backs, returned to the ambulance and pulled a long bed out of the back of the truck. As if by magic, legs with wheels attached dropped from under the bed and the men rolled the whole apparatus into the house.

For about five minutes, all was quiet. The men were all inside the house. The wailing noise was over and the moment felt suspendedto me. I stood at the window full of anticipation wondering what washappening inside our neighbor's house. Both vehicles seemed almost alive as their many lights were silently pulsing as if they too were watching and waiting with nervous anticipation. Then, in onesand twos, the men began to emerge. They were no longer hurryingas they strolled back toward their machines. Some were returning various pieces of equipment, none of which I recognized or understood, into compartments built into the outside of the trucks much like the storage areas beneath Niger busses. Others just gathered together and seemed to be hanging around, the tension gone from their bodies and from the situation I had observed a few minutes earlier.

Finally, the last two men came out of the house pushing the rollingbed that now carried a woman whom I recognized as a neighbor. She lay very still and rigid dressed in a rose colored shirt and was strapped firmly to the bed. The men moved quickly, but carefully, astwo other men broke off from their small group and joined them. Together, all four gently lifted her and slid her, bed and all, into theback of the ambulance, the legs once again retracting, as she entered her mobile hospital.

That was it. Two minutes later, everything was over as all the men returned to their original places except one who rode in the back withthe patient. Both trucks pulled away, lights flashing, but this time there was no wailing. I was still standing at the window, my Cheeriosgetting soggier by the minute, still staring at the spots where these giant machines had stood moments earlier, wondering what I had just seen. Eight men had arrived in two giant vehicles, each one equipped with life-saving tools and within minutes were gone carrying my neighbor away to what? I presumed to safety. I could nothelp but recall the most important of my own medical emergencies and the enormous difference in the response to it and to that of the neighbor's. If you feel sick in America, you don't even have to go by yourself, you can call an ambulance by dialing 911. It will come to pick you upand bring you to the hospital immediately. Plus, Americans have very qualified doctors.

In some parts of Niger, people don't even know what the word ambulance means. Most of the time they use traditional medicines tocure some diseases, but there are some diseases that have to be brought to the hospital. To bring someone sick on time to save them is very difficult in the desert. Sometimes, people have to carry the person on camelback a distance of twenty-five to forty-three kilometers to reach the nearest town. In my area, people can spend up to one or two days before they reach their destination depending on the sick person's condition. Most of the time, the person who runsthe hospital is going to give you some pills, because that is what there is. In fact, there is a good chance that the doctor may not evenbe there. Childbirth can also be complicated with healers. They can fail despite their knowledge of the subject. In some cases, either the baby or the mother dies. I remembered when one of my aunts was giving birth. She suffered a lot! My grandmother is a traditional healer. She tried everything she could to save her daughter, but shecouldn't. Her daughter passed away after giving birth to a handsomeboy who lived.

If we had had a clinic or an ambulance near where we lived in Niger,maybe my eye could have been saved when I was young. Maybe some of the medical tragedies in my family could have been prevented.

Technology and Convenience

There is no comparison of the availability of "things" in America to the availability of "things" in the Sahara. It is amazing to me how much Americans can acquire and how easily. If they want something, they don't even have leave their houses to go out to shop. Unbelievably, they can buy everything on-line with just a pushof a button. I have noticed that in America almost everything is doneby buttons. For example, opening garages, buying tickets and purchasing goods can often be accomplished by just pushing a button. In Niger, on the other hand, everything is done by ropes. Water has to be pulled up from our wells by rope and our tents are supported with ropes. Even our means of transportation, which is the camel, has to be led by a rope. Whereas the America may be a"button culture," Niger is definitely a "rope culture."

The tremendous convenience Americans have extends to their travel from place to place. To get directions in the United States is not a bigchallenge. Americans can travel to any place and be able to find it without using the sun or moon, as we must do when crossing the desert sand. They just consult a small device called a gps. We, nomads in Niger, work with stars at night and the sun during the dayto get directions.

And what about communication between peoples? The ease of communication in the United States is yet another source of amazement for me. People in America can receive letters, gifts or anything that can be sent through their mailbox by the postal service,Fed Ex or UPS. In the Sahara, on the other hand, we have no delivery services. If we want to deliver something, we have to deliverit ourselves. The problem is that we have only a 2% chance of finding the person to whom we want to send our communication. Wehave to deliver this communication to where we "think" he is. People are constantly moving around to seek a good pasture and water. Sometimes we learn that the person we are seeking has returned tothe area where we began our journey in the first place. Because there is no means of communication among travelers, we can easily miss someone and have to retrace our steps to find that person. When we have to repeat our journey again, it sometimes takes up totwo days on camelback.

Another surprising fact about travel in America is that you often haveto pay to use the highways that have been constructed to ease travel. However, there is an easy and absolutely astonishing way to pay those highway fees. That realization gave me a headache. For example, when I traveled in the Mini Cooper with my host family in the United States, I saw Doug, the driver and my host "father," pull up to the toll gate and pass right on through without stopping. I knewhe was supposed to pay, but he rolled right through the gate. I had ahard time believing it, because I didn't see how or where the money was paid from the device that was located on the car windshield. Themagic part of this EZ-pass is that, even if the car is going fast, the EZ-pass is able to suck the money from the device in the car.

I decided to ask my energetic friend Doug about this magic. He said that the paying process was all done by electronic transfers. Then, deep in my mind, I wondered what would happen if this device brokedown. Doug added a very magical statement. He said that even if this device runs out of money, the money will be replenished from hiscredit card. I said to myself, "Are these people working with ghosts or what is going on in this part of the planet?" "Mamaqui," I thought to myself in Tuareg, which means, "I am speechless." One day I experienced another ghostly presence when Doug stopped at a store and put his card into a machine that gave birth to money. I had no idea where it found money. I also wondered how it gave the right amount. I was told that it was called an ATM. I tried to understand it, but to me it seemed like money was just shooting out from a metal refrigerator.

Another example of my astonishment was when I first saw the microwave in the kitchen of my host family. As I approached it, it looked like a cooler or a game machine. However, I found that it was there to cook food and to cook it very fast. I don't know how. It doesn't smoke when it cooks like the cooking fires I am accustomed to. I tried to see where the fire was coming from, but I couldn't. What I saw were two circles that look like speakers on each side of the machine. However, I didn't hear any music playing from these speakers. Even today, after cooking many pizzas and macaroni andcheese dinners in that microwave, I still don't have any idea about how it cooks food.

I received yet another great surprise when I asked my friend Doug about the music in his iPhone. He had turned it on as we were driving in the car. Doug explained that the music is stored in a cloud.I hardly believed it, because for me only rainfall is stored in the clouds. I wondered who could leave music in a cloud. And how? For me, it is another amazing miracle because music is not an object. We cannot touch it, so how can it be stored?

It reminded me of one of my earliest memories of electronic devices,the first time I saw a radio. My uncle Amoumane had a radio and he liked to listen to the news in the Hausa language, because he didn't speak French or any western languages. My friends and I were about seven years old and we were very surprised to hear people speaking within the radio. We had no idea how that was possible! Sounds and speech were coming out of a box. We laughed at thosestrange voices.

One morning we went to his tent to help his wife tie the small camelsso that they wouldn't follow their mothers for milk. When we finished our task, we went inside the tent and saw the radio under the bed. I decided to hold it in my hands trying to look inside. We wanted to see whether there were people in there or not. One of my friends said, "Why are they not talking now?" I replied, "I don't know. Maybethey are still sleeping." Then my friend Ghoumar said "Maybe they don't have anything to say today and I think they know that we don't speak their language." After a moment my uncle arrived from the well. We decided to ask him and he explained to us. He said that there were no people inside, but rather a bunch of wires connectedwith each other. Actually he himself was fascinated about the miracle, but he had decided to accept it as so because he was an adult. Whenever I enter a movie theatre in the United States, I remember the first time I saw a movie in the town of Arlit back in Niger. What acontrast! It was during the time my mother decided to take me to another school in the Dannat area. We had to pass by Arlit in order to find a car that would go to Dannat. When we arrived at Arlit, we stayed with some relatives that lived in the most remote place in thetown. They didn't have electricity. Everything was dark, but then, asa desert dweller, I was used to the dark. What I was going to experience would be quite different.

One night, one of the children of the house invited me to see a moviewith him. I couldn't imagine what that would be like, but I grabbed some coins from my mother and we headed to the "movie theatre." In the darkness, we could see the French company compound far away in the night. There were many lights illuminating the area.

As we approached the "movie theatre," I could see children runningaround and trying to get in, in order to find a nice seat inside. The "theatre" was a small straw hut in the middle of town. When my friend and I arrived at the door, we found the owner standing still at the entrance waiting to collect the admission fee from each viewer. The fee to see one movie was 25F CFA ($0.01). He started by collecting coins from the children. I didn't really know much about money at the time, because I hadn't used money when I was growing up in the desert. The children from the town did know a bit about profit. There were some children who set out bowls of peanutsin front of the straw hut in order to sell them to the movie goers. Other children swooped in to buy the peanuts and then headed intothe straw hut with their tasty treats. Once we were inside, the film immediately started without any commercials. There were no previews or commercials like those shown in American theaters. There were no chairs in the hut, just arug that had been laid on the sand. We all dropped down on the rugcrowded together in a heap of energetic bodies. Soon, we settled down to watch the film.

It was difficult to fully enjoy the movie, because the wind was fiercely blowing outside and it streamed through the straw with a low buzz. Often during the viewing, the electricity would fade in and out. Also, the quality of the presentation was poor. We had to keep squinting atthe screen, because the image was so blurred. Due to the rolling sand seeping into the hut, the screen sometimes seemed to be shimmering mirage. The speakers were full of sand and were wrapped in tape so the sound was also muffled. Nevertheless, when the movie started, we all fell silent, in anticipation of this new miracle. The first image I saw on the screen was a flying, white horse that appeared at the beginning of the movie. I had never seen a horse flybefore, and he was flying at me. I raised my arms to protect myself from this danger. There were also other surprises for me in this first movie. Whenever I saw someone choking another person on screen,I would close my eyes, because I didn't like to see anyone dying. I couldn't stop wondering why were these people killing each other. I said to myself, " If these people continue killing each other like this, they will wipe out humanity." I tried to ask kids around me about the film and what was happening, but they didn't understand my language. I would touch someone and try to talk to him loudly aboutwhat was going on in the movie. However, not understanding my Tuareg language, those around me would often gesture to me to bequiet. But I needed someone to explain to me why those people were killing each other, because I knew there had to be a reason. Four years later, I learned that that first movie was called "Rambo" and that Rambo was a hero, and his killing was the killing of "bad guys." This was a new concept, but since then Rambo has becomeone of my favorite films.

My first movie experience in the United States could not have beenmore different. The movie theatre was giant, well equipped and air conditioned. There were large TV screens hanging advertising different upcoming movies or flashing commercials for various products. The floors were so clean that I could see my reflection in their shine and gloss. All around me I saw well-dressed people rushing into different rooms to see their favorite movies. In one building you could see 14 different movies! The smell of popcorn was everywhere. The movie screen was as large as our entire straw hut movie theatre back in Arlit and was so clear that I sometimes hadthe impression that I was in the movie. I often found myself avoiding some objects from the film. Those objects and shapes looked so real you could almost feel their presence. In the middle of the 3D movie, Lifeof Pi, there was a ship accident in which all the animals on board were cast into the sea. There was a huge herd of zebras that headedright towards the audience, frantically moving their legs and paddlingforward. I found myself trying to avoid them, hunching my shoulders and drawing myself far back into my seat. It was so real I thought Icould smell the flesh of zebra, the scent of ocean.

Another example of the use of technology in America is in the schools. I have seen some of these schools both in Scottsdale and in New Hampshire. Most of them are immense, tidy and comfortable.When you look at one of them from far away, it looks like a whole neighborhood. I was very shocked by the size of classrooms and recreation fields. The students have absolutely everything they need to achieve their goals. They are taught by very well trained teachers and have electricity and the Internet in their schools. What surprised me the most is that everyone has access to a computer, and there isa wireless connection almost everywhere within the school. It's very easy for students to be in touch with their teachers to ask them questions. Students are also able to help each other on-line and exchange their thoughts about their courses. Schools own buses for transporting students to their homes and bringing them back to school again. Students can practice any kind of sport, including American football, in their schools as they have huge fields.

I was surprised almost every day by the discovery of another technological device in the United States. Some of it seemed likemagic to me, but I did not see the same sense of wonder in my American friends. The biggest surprise to me was that I seemed tobe the only one who was surprised.

Social Interaction

I have discovered that Americans are always in a hurry and seem toalways want to be somewhere else rather than where they are. Theyalso seem to communicate little with one another when they are rushing about. I was surprised to see people not greeting one another. Even when they come to a crosswalk, they often don't wait until the crossing signal turns to white. They repeatedly push the pedestrian button and think by pushing the button the light will change faster. Miraculously, the button often talks to them saying, "please wait," but they don't. They just keep pushing and pushing toget across.

The ones driving cars seem to see the red lights as a great inconvenience and a waste of time. Although they are sometimes very kind to me when I bike, waving me across an intersection, I alsosee them rushing through yellow lights before they turn red. It's as if something were pulling them ahead magnetically. I always wonder why they are in such a hurry. Where are they all going?

I thought once I started using public transportation, I would be out in the community and would make some friends. However, I experienced the opposite situation. When I climbed onto the bus and sat down, I saw that everyone had earphones on, and they were all busy manipulating their cell phones. They didn't even pay attention to the person next to them. I usually say hello to the person next to me, but most of the time they don't respond. It seems as if they haveleft their minds somewhere else and only their bodies are riding on the bus. They seem to be rushing to do or speak about other things and not present to interact with one another in the moment. Sometimes, they just flash you a very tiny smile in response to a greeting, but it is rare. When they get off, it's the same silence. Theydon't say goodbye to you, but, fortunately, at least they thank the driver.

More surprisingly, families here don't spend much time together. For example, if you ask someone how long it has been since he saw his parents or his children, he might say one or two years. According to my observation, people here spend more time at work than they do with their children. The problem is, even if they get together, they don't seem to talk a great deal with each other. Rather they just concentrate on their phones or computers. Instead of laughing together, they laugh into their phones. Instead of exchanging news ofthe day, they read the news on their mobile devices. Sometimes I have the impression that phones and computers are their best friends. There are exceptions. My first birthday celebration ever wasextraordinary and unforgettable.

First of all, as a nomad, I didn't even know the exact date of my birth.It's a challenge for us nomads to tell the exact day and month of our birthdays. First, we are not born in a hospital where records can be kept. Second, we don't observe the Gregorian calendar of the Western World. We determine our birthdays according to some special event, such as a drought, that happened at the time of birth. For example, I was born three years after President Kountche, the president of Niger, died. That's as close as I can come to knowing the date of my birth. In the U.S., I needed a birth date and had decided to record my birthday date as a date based on the Berber calendar. Respondingto that decision, my host family decided they would organize a birthday party for me.

I remember when Doug and I were sitting in the backyard talking about birthday parties in American communities. He explained to me how important it is to celebrate birthdays and that it's part of the culture. I had attended several birthday parties in the city of Niamey where I went to high school. I found them so interesting that I alwayswished to have one for myself one day. Now it would happen.

Doug told me that he had invited some of his friends for the occasion. I felt so happy to know that these people were coming just for my birthday party and to meet me. I said to myself, "Wow despitepeople rushing in all directions here in the U.S., they still do have time for one another." However, I was also nervous. I didn't know what to expect.

The day arrived, and Mousa, my friend from Niger who is now livingin Tucson, came to celebrate my birthday a la americana. He had come with his wife, Christina, who was eight months pregnant with their daughter. Mousa had taken me in his car to pick up another friend in Gilbert, AZ. Together we pulled up to my host family's housefor the party. As we drove up to the entrance, I was surprised by the number of cars parked in front of the house. I had never seen cars there before.Usually, in this neighborhood, the roadway was vacant, and all cars were parked in the adjacent garages. Now something unusual was happening. Additionally, there were two balloons bobbing up and down in the entrance way. One said, "Happy Birthday," and the otherread, "It's a Boy." Hey, that was me!

We climbed out of Mousa's car and walked up to the front door. I felt very nervous by this time. I was not used to being the center of attention. What would this be like? What did a birthday party involve?Why were there so many cars out front? I tried to calm down. "It can'tbe dangerous," I told myself. "It should be something good." I was also a bit disturbed because of another problem. In the Islamic faith, we don't acknowledge birthdays. Now, I was living in a differentculture where birthdays were recognized and celebrated. I was againbridging these two different worlds.

As we opened the door to the house, I saw many faces I had never seen before, smiling at me and wishing me a "Happy Birthday." I began to walk forward into the group and to meet the different people there, shaking hands and repeating my name to them. I felt agrowing comfort among these guests and experienced a new sense of welcome and belonging. They knew who I was and wanted me to feel celebrated. Now I would participate in the rituals of that celebration. There was ahuge birthday cake on the table in the middle of the living room. It was covered with white and chocolate icing, and there were twenty-two candles sticking up from the top. The candles were lit with tiny flames, and the people around me sang the song, "Happy Birthday to you. Happy Birthday to you. Happy Birthday, dear Ahmed. HappyBirthday to you." Then they told me to blow the candles out, and I did. And everyone clapped.

After eating cake and ice cream, my host Doug directed me to a place in the living room where there was a large stack of gifts… gifts for me, all wrapped up with ribbons. I sat on a chair and began to open them as one of the neighbors told me whom each gift was fromso I could thank them. It was amazing. I received candy, clothes, giftcards for McDonald's and I-tunes and movies, and a pair of gloves from my host mother so I wouldn't freeze my hands when I rode theirbike. I couldn't believe all this. As I look back on that day, it is hard to appreciate and to understandthe generosity of that day. The day of my birthday party, I only knewa few people in my new community in Scottsdale, but I had never seen the rest of them before. They took their time and decided to come to a nomad's birthday. Everyone brought me a gift, and each of them smiled at me. They really made me feel more comfortable than ever. I also came to realize that no matter what part of the globeI might visit, people still have a sense of community, and they do care for one another.

Two Worlds

My immersion into the American culture has accounted for only a small fraction of the time I have lived. For the most part, my thoughtsand beliefs have been formed by Tuareg and other Niger cultures. After arriving in America, I was exposed to so much, so fast, that I often found myself thinking of, and thanking, my grandfather who taught me to accept change while staying calm. I found that I had to make adjustments to my expectations every day. Almost nothing wasfamiliar to me.

Even something that is as simple as greeting another person wasstartlingly different. There were no multiple handshakes anymore. Whenever I meet someone in Niger we expect to shake hands manytimes, but in America people hardly shake hands once. Amongst mypeople, anytime that you meet someone you shake hands until the greetings end. This can take a while. We usually ask how each person is doing, his camels, etc.

Another surprise for me was a hand gesture that sometimes still getsme confused. In Niger, if someone raises his hand towards you and spreads his fingers it means an insult similar in meaning to a single- digit gesture seen in America. Americans do that spread-finger waveas a greeting. It is not an insult for them. I have often received unintended insults from people that I met and it took me some getting used to before I came to see the humor in it.

It seems that people in America have many choices about everything, but they still seem to crave more and to be dissatisfied agreat deal of the time. I have to admit, this desire for needs and services is contagious. I have been guilty of the same feelings. I have searched phone plans so that I can communicate with my family in Niger. And, surprising to me, I have complained about the efficiency or ease of acquiring such technologies. I find myself almost losing those memories of wonder because of the new world Ihave encountered. I then have to remind myself about where I comefrom and what is available to my people, which are just the basic necessities of life.

Even eating in a restaurant in the United States is a totally different experience. In Niger, it is common that the restaurant owner is at thesame time the waiter, the cook and the dishwasher. One of the few times that I ate in a restaurant in Niger, there wasn't a menu, which is common. When we finished eating, the owner brought two cups and showed us the water container. In Niger, electricity is a luxury not everybody has. He didn't have electricity and there was no cold running water. Instead he had a jar that was covered with some sortof bag that kept it cooler. We filled our cups several times.

In Niger, I wasn't really worried about bacteria, but in the United States I learned to worry about it. I have become aware of germs. It's true. Although I never worried about microbes in Niger, in the UnitedStates I began to always be aware of bacteria. The saying back in Niger is, "A microbe or pathogen must be as large as a donkey to killan African." Now I am worried about all those microbes that are so small I can't even see them. Is danger all around me? Have I lost mystrength? Have I surrendered to the fear of tiny specks in my environment? Am I still the same "African" who can only be killed by a pathogen as large as a donkey? What have I gained and what have I lost?

Whenever I now wait impatiently at the bus stop you would think thatI would recall our only transportation back deep in the desert, the one that takes us from our village to Arlit where we can connect to the intra-city bus. It was an old Toyota pickup truck, the same one that failed to arrive in time to save my eye earlier in my life. It would usually arrive full of goats and people. Sometimes, you had to sit among the goats and just be patient as they pushed up against you or even climbed over you until you finally got to town. Sometimes it might take as many as two days to get to Arlit because the truck would break down or have successive flat tires. That's why we calledit, "bring your meal, you never know." How can I forget this so easily? And, still, I find myself getting impatient. How can I forget that I once had to walk fifty-four kilometers (33+ miles) across the desert because there was no other choice? How did this change in me happen? What do I need to learn in order to find some balance? Is iteven possible to find balance?

Recently, I have been imagining what it would have been like if I would have been born in America into a family, my family, if they hadlived in America for generations instead of being Tuaregs in the Sahara. What would be my present reality? I can imagine my grandfather being a famous poet having retired by now, playing golfinstead of herding camels. I also imagine one of my uncles, the onewho enjoys mixing things all the time, as a famous chemist. With no formal education at any level, he can maintain his flashlight batteriesfor months just by adding salty water and other mixtures.

What has become plain to me, after having the opportunity to live intwo worlds, is that they are who they are and we all are who we areand that our identities are largely determined by the realities, both cultural and physical, in which we have been immersed during our lives. Life in the desert is hard, but also full of love, cooperation, music, laughter and profound lessons. I am reminded of the proverbmy grandfather taught us, "God created countries with much water for men to live in and He created deserts for men to discover their souls." What I have to determine is what will happen to me now that I havebeen a nomad immersed in two completely different worlds.

Conclusion

Over this past year, we have watched with interest and admiration asAhmed has explored and negotiated a world that could not have been more different than the one he left behind. Ahmed is someone who had lived without the basic things Americans take for granted: water, electricity… a bed. But he now has figured out how to use anolder model phone without a Sim card to make calls, listen to news programs in French, conduct research and interact with a Friends ofTuaregs group on Facebook. Clearly, he possesses problem solvingskills that should bode well for his future.

Yet, consider his situation. Ahmed has become a nomad in two worlds. His problem, as he articulates it, is that he "can't inhabit bothworlds at the same time" and he now feels he is being pulled in two directions. He has said: "I think I have to be careful not to put both ofmy feet into the modern world. As we Tuaregs say, 'If you put one foot into the modern world, you are tempted; if you put both into it you are lost.' I don't want to be 'lost' and to abandon my traditional lifestyle. It is what made me who I am today. But, today, I am not among my people and my life is good in the United States. It may be different…in fact, it is completely different…but I love it also."

He has been asked if he knew the song that goes "How ya gonna keep 'em down on the farm once they've seen Paree'?" Of course, he had never heard it before, but he clearly understands why he hadbeen asked that question and even more clearly saw how the sentiment applies to his situation. He may have seen too much to return to the desert full time. There is so much to learn, to see, to do,to enjoy, in short, to love about a modern life in a technologically advanced world. From what I can see living in the same house with him, there is not a waking minute that he is not engaged in what it offers. Life as a nomad in the desert is exhausting and dangerous; it leaveslittle time for pursuits that are not adapted for desert survival. A culture that must engage in life at the survival level does not have the time and resources necessary to develop the technology that might free them from subsistence-level living. That is the reality for his people along with opportunism of foreign powers, destructive development threatening a fragile ecology and the incessant southward advance of desertification from climate change in the Sahara. Real, lasting, and timely solutions are not going to be foundfrom within the culture. Ahmed's greatest hope is to bring solutions from the developed world that can benefit his people. He has to find a way to reconcile his two worlds: to be able to contribute to his native community while learning the ways of modern society. Yet, forhim, a clear path to accomplish these goals remains unclear.

Ahmed has come to the conclusion that education must be an important part of his solution. He has coined a term that captures theessence of the dilemma. "I have come to see that I will have to become a 'semi-nomad' in order for me to keep my two worlds. The truth is I can't live without either of them anymore. I'm becoming a mixture of these two 'planets' and the only way to balance them is tocontinue to learn. And that, I hope, will allow me to learn from one in order to bring solutions to the other."

Doug Fallon

Mary Fallon

Special Thanks

I don't want to finish this book without giving my special thanks to Bess Palmisciano. She is the executive director of the non- governmental organization, Rain for Sahel and Sahara, and has dedicated her life and time to the nomadic people (Tuaregs and Wadaabe) in Niger to help us survive. Rain has aided my people by improving education, increasing gardening, digging wells and more. Bess arranged for me to come to the United States for my eye surgery, for which I am grateful every day. I consider Bess to be a family member and she is one of the people who have motivated meto want to find ways to help my nomadic communities.

I want to thank Mary and Doug Fallon, my host family in America, fornot only taking me into their home but also for being my teachers. They helped me to adjust to American life, they taught me English and they spent countless hours mentoring me through the writing of this book.

Ahmed Kemil